THE IOWA WRITERS' WORKSHOP COOKBOOK

* * *

Edited by
Connie Brothers

Illustrated by
Peter Nelson

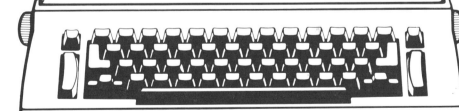

FREDERICK FELL PUBLISHERS, INC.   HOLLYWOOD, FL

I want to acknowledge the valuable assistance provided by my friends John Leggett, Nancy Hamilton, Larry Eckholt, Jim Harris, Mercer Warriner, Sheryl Christensen Galvez, and Sue Loring, without which this cookbook would not have been possible.

International Standard Book Number: 0-8119-0690-6
Library of Congress Catalog Card Number: 84-081711

For information address:

Frederick Fell Publishers, Inc.
2500 Hollywood Blvd.
Hollywood, Fla. 33020

Published simultaneously in Canada by:
Book Center, Inc.
Montreal

MANUFACTURED IN THE UNITED STATES OF AMERICA

1 2 3 4 5 6 7 8 9 0

Photographs on pages 138 and 142 courtesy of Wayne Engineering;
photograph on page 68 courtesy of Bio-Rad Laboratories, Inc., Digilab Division

CONTENTS

When asked why she chose to write about food rather than "the struggle for power and security, and about love, the way others do," M.F.K. Fisher replied:

> "The easiest answer is to say that, like most other humans, I am hungry. But there is more than that. It seems to me that our three basic needs, for food and security and love, are so mixed and mingled and entwined that we cannot straightly think of one without the other. So it happens that when I write about hunger, I am really writing about love and the hunger for it, and warmth and the love of it and the hunger for it...and then the warmth and richness and fine reality of hunger satisfied...and it is all one."

INTRODUCTION

Writers tend to have a lot of spare time to think about food. They often prefer to think about anything at all rather than face the novel, story or poem which is at that moment frustrating them. Writers frequently work at home and use cooking to avoid their work, the demon wrestling that is part of the creative process. Whenever an author imagines a character in a novel eating something, it's possible that whatever the character eats is what the writer aspires to for his or her own lunch.

Here are the recipes of 120 American writers associated with the Iowa Writers' Workshop. Some write poetry and some write fiction, but in either case a good poem or story will be like a good recipe, with the proper ingredients, hopefully fresh, in the right proportions, rendered with care to create the intended effect.

Peter Nelson
Connie Brothers

* * *

SOUPS

* * *

Chicken Soup

Laurie Colwin

This is really poached chicken. It is very pure and delicious and should be used as invalid food. It is perfect as the first real food after an illness.

Ingredients *(for two or three people)*

2 whole chicken breasts split into four parts. Skin and every shred of fat should be removed
2 medium onions peeled and cut into four pieces
1 large carrot (the larger the sweeter) cut into five good-size pieces
8 peppercorns
1 strip of lemon peel (a potato peeler does this job well) about 3 inches long

1. Put the peppercorns in the bottom of a small enamel kettle. Do not use aluminum or iron. Add the onion and carrot. Place the chicken pieces on top of the vegetables and add the lemon peel.
2. Add bottled water to barely cover. Tap water can be used unless it has a decided taste.
3. Put on the lowest possible heat and allow to simmer gently for at least two hours. This soup cannot overcook.
4. Serve in a soup plate with knife and fork, and toast.
5. For those who like celery, use one stalk of celery cut in five pieces for this dish.

Sopa de Pollo—Mexico City

(an archeological find!)

Kathleen Fraser

I first tasted this crisp, hot, lemony soup as a "specialty of the house" in a discrete restaurant housed in a large and modern hotel near the Archeological Museum in Mexico City. I was enormously pleased and surprised by its visual presentation and by the combination of this zesty soup, afloat with big chunks of chicken breast, each bowl lavishly garnished with finely cut radishes and iceberg lettuce on one side and a piece of ripe avocado on the other. The soup was fresh-looking and summery in its colors and definitely a meal in itself, served with warm corn tortillas, cold Mexican beer, and fresh pineapple for dessert.

I have since improvised my own version, which I believe to be very close to the original. It is *always* a big hit. People love to spoon down through the layers.

Iceberg lettuce
Radishes, firm and bright red
1–2 ripe avocadoes (depending
   on size)
   Chopped parsley
Lemon slices, or lime slices
2 cans chicken broth (or 4 cups
   homemade broth, leftover
   from stewed chicken)
2–4 chicken breasts (boned and
   skinned after poaching)
1 small can chopped mild green
   chiles, with tomato
Juice of 1 lemon (more or less,
   to taste)
Tabasco sauce, several shakes
   (to taste, but it should add a
   peppery zip)

Poach the chicken breasts
in the broth, green chilies,

Tabasco, and parsley until tender. Don't overcook. Add the juice of a fresh lemon. Finely slice the lettuce and radishes (like *very* fine shoestring potatoes) and arrange them on a platter with pieces of avocado (⅓ to ¼ of the avocado is a good size). Serve the soup from a tureen with lemon or lime slices floating on top. Compose each bowl at the table with the fresh vegetables from the serving platter.

Shrimp Bisque

Mark Helprin

In a large saucepan place as many shrimp as you can afford, deveined and shelled. Add one 6½-ounce can of solid white tuna in water (crumbled with a fork). Cover with water and boil vigorously for 5 minutes. Season with red pepper, garlic, white wine, and dill. After 4 minutes add 1 quart water, 1 quart skim milk, and 1 large bunch of watercress, including the stems, slightly chopped. Take 5 or 6 Italian tomatoes and cut into quarters. Throw them in. Add ¾ stick of butter and ½ cup of white wine. Reduce from boil and simmer for a few minutes. While stirring add paprika.

Serve with black bread, smoked salmon, lemon wedges, and beer. Serves 4.

Chili

Jane Howard

Here's a good, fast chili recipe I recently devised:

Sauté 2 large chopped onions with 2 or 3 chopped cloves of garlic. Add 2 pounds or more of chopped beef; sauté together briefly. Add a can of tomato purée, half a cup or so of Texas or Oklahoma barbeque sauce, 2 or 3 chopped carrots, 4 or 5 chopped celery stalks, ¼ cup or so of celery seeds, 2 cans each of kidney and garbanzo beans, and chili powder to taste.

Experiment, if you like, with quantities. This keeps well and can be frozen.

One of my dreams, along with returning to live permanently in Iowa City, is to never have to eat another homecooked meal. Ann and I manage to eat out about two-thirds of the time. I like Mexican food, Greek food, and Polish food. I hate dates, figs, lasagna, eggplant, and anything that has been even remotely close to a fish.

On the rare occasions when I cook I make pizza (I once

operated a restaurant called Caesar's Italian Village), tapioca pudding, or

Bologna Soup

W.P. (Bill) Kinsella

8 ounces tomato juice
8 ounces whole milk
3 slices of bologna

Place tomato juice in a saucepan, heat, adding ⅛ teaspoon of baking soda. Stir. Add milk. Dice bologna and add to mixture. No need to cook, simply heat and season to taste with black pepper. Parsley or basil may be added if desired.

Cream of Zucchini Soup

Carol Muske

A little butter, a little oil in a heavy skillet. Watch till it foams—add 4 or 5 sliced zucchini, *thinly* sliced. Sauté till golden, glistening even. I forgot, you're supposed to slice and sauté onions too, 2 medium size. When *both* zucchini and onions are golden, purée or blend or cuisinartize till fairly smooth in texture. Replace in skillet, add 2½ cups chicken broth plus a little water, or stock, stir, simmer. Add salt and white pepper to taste. Simmer a while. Before serving, stir in ½ cup or so of heavy cream. Float 3 or 4 sliced zukes on top of soup. Serve hot or cold.

Shadow Soup

Peter Nelson

Put the manuscript you're working on in the refrigerator, where it will be safe if your house catches fire. Ideally, it should be a weepy autobiographical first novel about thwarted love, but any mother/daughter or father/son tragedy will do, or two nihilist postholocaust novellas.

Get in an old station wagon with a dent in the right front fender and drive to a supermarket. Purchase the least expensive uncut chicken you can find with your last remaning food stamps. Take it home and set it somewhere your dog can't reach while you check your mail, first putting an even gallon of water on the stove to boil. Season water to taste with salt, pepper, or little packets of ketchup stolen from fast food restaurants.

Remove chicken from package. Put a glove on your right hand, and make sure you're wearing a long sleeved shirt. Once the water is boiling, turn on the overhead light. It should be a bare 60-watt bult—100 watts are better, but they're expensive. Take the chicken in your right hand and dangle it over the boiling water, allowing the shadow to play upon the roiling surface for thirty minutes. Keep the chicken close to the water, ensuring a good dark shadow. Re-wrap the chicken and put it in the refrigerator where your manuscript was. Take the manuscript out and re-read it as you drink the water. Look out the window at your car and sigh. Serves one young writer.

Soup

Grace Paley

Cook   ¾ cup split peas
        ½ cup lentils
        ¼ cup barley
in a pot of water and add a couple
onions and a couple stalks
of celery with all the greens—
cut into a couple pieces so you
can eat it later. (When I was
growing up we used to throw
out the celery.)

Let it go for an hour till the peas and lentils are soft and mushy. Add 3 or 4 carrots and cook till done. Sometimes I add a little tamari and sometimes I add a can of whole tomatoes or fresh tomatoes.

When you serve it, add ½ cup peas or zucchini. It's important never to let the carrots get too soft. Never.

14

Portuguese Kale and Linguica Soup

Sherod Santos

1 cup dried red kidney beans
½ pound kale, *or* one 10-ounce
   box frozen kale, thawed
2 medium onions, chopped fine
3 cloves garlic, minced
4 medium potatoes, peeled and
   diced
8 cups chicken broth
3 cups drained canned Italian
   tomatoes, roughly chopped
1 bay leaf
1 teaspoon salt
¾ pound linguica or chorizo
   sausage
Pepper

1. Soak beans overnight in water. (*Or:* cover beans with water in a large saucepan and bring to a boil. Boil for 1 minute, cover, turn off heat, and let beans sit for 1 hour.) Bring the beans to a boil, reduce to a simmer, and cook uncovered until beans are tender, 2 to 3 hours.

2. Wash the kale and strip the leaves from the stem. Chop very fine. If using frozen kale, squeeze out excess liquid and chop very fine.

3. Heat oil in a large stockpot. Sauté the onions over medium-low heat until soft and translucent. Add the minced garlic for the last minute, or until the flavor comes.

4. Add potatoes, broth, tomatoes, bay leaf, and salt and bring to a boil. Reduce to a simmer and cook, partially covered, until the potatoes are very soft, about 20 minutes.

5. With a wooden spoon, mash most of the potatoes against the side of the stockpot to make a coarse purée.

6. Prick the sausages, place them in a skillet, and cover with water. Bring to a boil, reduce to a simmer, and cook uncovered for 15 minutes. Drain on paper towels and slice into ¼-inch rounds.

7. Bring the soup to a boil and reduce to a simmer. Add the kale and simmer for 5 minutes. Add the sausage and the beans and simmer for a few minutes until heated through. Remove the bay leaf. Check for salt and pepper. Serves 6.

K.B.'s Cold Blueberry Soup

W.D. Snodgrass

2 1-pound cans of blueberries in
   syrup
1½ cups water
3 lemon slices
1 teaspoon black pepper,
   freshly ground
1 teaspoon allspice, freshly
   ground
½ teaspoon cloves, freshly
   ground
Dash of nutmeg
1 tablespoon sugar
½ tablespoon flour
2 tablespoons cold water
½ cup sour cream
¼ cup light cream
Whipped cream garnish

Bring blueberries, 1½ cups water, lemon slices, pepper, allspice, cloves, nutmeg, and sugar to a boil; simmer 15 minutes. Press through a fine sieve and return to the stove. Add flour dissolved in 2 tablespoons cold water. Simmer until liquid is slightly thickened. Cool. Add sour cream and light cream. Chill. Serve with a dollop of whipped cream in each bowl.

Lentil Soup

Robert Stone

10 cups water or soup stock
½ pound lentils
2 ribs celery
2 carrots
1 great big onion or two
   middle-sized ones
1 clove garlic
1 8-ounce can tomato sauce
¼ cup olive oil
Salt and pepper to taste

Boil water, add lentils, and simmer for an hour. Chop up vegetables and garlic and add to soup, along with tomato sauce and olive oil. At this point, I add seasonings to suit my mood—such as Tabasco, bay leaf, paprika. Cook for another 30—45 minutes. This is best when cooked one day before you are going to eat it because it improves with age. Leave it out of the refrigerator overnight (within reason).

Essential Chili

Dan Wakefield

Writing is a lonely, introspective business and can easily lead to despair. One surefire way to stave it off is to call up a dozen friends or so and invite them over for chili. Tell them to bring a jug of wine and some beer, and you'll provide the chili. All you have to do is get a big pot, put it on the stove,

17

put on some music, start sipping a little wine, and do the following. Slice up 2 large onions and brown them in the pot with some butter or margarine. Then put in 2 pounds of hamburger and mash it around till it is brown too. Pour on a lot of chili powder, then add 2 large cans of peeled tomatoes and 6 regular-size cans of kidney beans, and cook the whole thing about an hour. Serve with big hunks of bread, partake of the wine or beer, and think how good it is to be alive and have food to eat and friends to share it with!

I consumed huge amounts of good chili when I taught at Iowa the wonderful spring semester of 1972, and began my novel *Starting Over* in a farmhouse in West Branch. I now live in Boston and make chili on Beacon Hill, where I finished my last novel, *Under The Apple Tree.*

* * *

BREADS

* * *

Old Iowa Cranberry Bread

Joe David Bellamy

Here is a recipe for cranberry bread that I hate to give up; but in the interest of humankind in general and of making a good cookbook, I felt I should be willing to part with something of consequence.

1 cup unbleached white flour
1 cup whole wheat flour
¼ cup bran
1 cup sugar
1½ teaspoon baking powder
½ teaspoon soda

1 egg, beaten
2 tablespoons oil or melted butter
1 orange—juice and grated rind

Add enough water to egg, juice, and shortening to make ¾ cup liquid

2 cups halved cranberries (can be frozen)
½ cup walnuts or pecans

Stir dry ingredients together.
Stir in liquid just enough to moisten.
Fold in cranberries and nuts.
Bake in small loaf pan in a 375° oven about 35 minutes—or until toothpick comes out clean.
This bread is especially appropriate for use by writers on sub-zero days when the sumac is encased in icicles. You place the Old Iowa Cranberry Bread on a blue saucer next to your manuscript or computer screen, and it helps you through an otherwise bitter afternoon. Words come leaping to the tongue.

Dubie's Corn and Cheese Bread

Norman Dubie

1 cup flour
1 cup yellow cornmeal
3 teaspoons baking powder
1 teaspoon salt
1 egg (beat some)
2 tablespoons Vermont
   maple syrup
1 cup milk
¼ cup corn oil
½ cup chopped mushrooms
1 cup corn
½ cup grated Vermont
   Store cheese
8-inch square pan
375° oven
30-35 minutes baking time

1. Mix flour, baking powder, salt, and cornmeal.
2. Stir maple syrup, egg, and milk together.
3. Heat the corn oil in a small pan and add the mushrooms. You can add a teaspoon of beer if you like. Sauté over medium heat for 6 minutes. Then the mushrooms and oil should be allowed to cool for 5 minutes.
4. Add the milk preparation to the cornmeal preparation and blend well.
5. Add corn, mushrooms with all the oil from the pan, and the grated sharp cheese. Now combine thoroughly.
6. Empty into well-greased pan. Bake until golden brown.

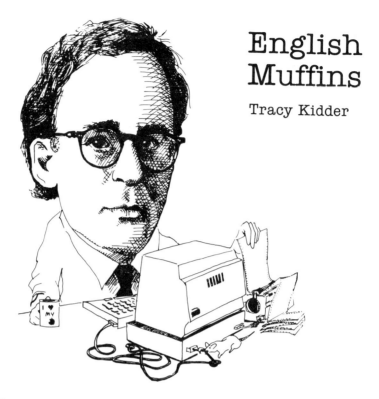

English Muffins

Tracy Kidder

I don't cook much, but my favorite recipe is for English muffins. I slice the muffin in two, none too carefully—I don't care if I use a fork or a knife. Then I pop both halves in the toaster and wait. Afterward, I smear things on them. Butter usually, sometimes jam, every so often peanut butter, maybe cream cheese or tuna fish. I think that a nice Bordeaux goes well with muffins of any sort, not, as a rule, one of the classified clarets, but a robust cru bourgeois, of a good vintage.

Squash Bread

Maxine Kumin

In the fallen month of February in New Hampshire, we usually find ourselves custodians of some winter squashes that are beginning to fail. One pleasant way of dealing with them is to make squash bread.

This will make 2 loaves in ordinary breadloaf pans; 3 if you fill them less full. The loaves are very dense.

Beat 4 medium, or 3 extra-large eggs together with 1 cup vegetable oil and 1½ cups of sugar (you can substitute maple syrup for part or all of the sugar, if you have a glut of this commodity). Do this in a very large bowl, then sift directly onto it 3 cups of flour, 1 teaspoon baking powder, 2 teaspoons baking soda, 1 teaspoon salt, 1 teaspoon cinnamon, 1 teaspoon nutmeg, 1 teaspoon ginger. You can omit ginger if you don't like the flavor, or substitute a little ground cloves. Mix well. Then stir in 2 cups of cooked squash that you have either buzzed smooth in the blender or in a food processor, or sieved through a food mill. Lastly, add 2 cups of raisins and 1 cup of chopped nuts which you have mixed together with ⅓ cup of flour. (This procedure will more or less keep them from sinking to the bottom of the batter while baking.) Bake in ungreased pans in a 350° oven for 1 hour, at least. Test with a toothpick for doneness; they may need another 20 minutes or so, depending on how moist or dry you like your bread, and how full the pans were.

Blueberry Muffins

Tim O'Brien

½ cup butter
1 cup sugar
2 eggs
1½ teaspoon vanilla
2 teaspoons baking powder
½ teaspoon salt
2 cups flour
½ cup milk
2½ cups fresh blueberries
2 teaspoons sugar

Cream shortening with sugar. Beat eggs and put those in. Mix well for about 3 minutes. Add vanilla and beat for about a minute. Combine all dry ingredients (baking powder, salt, and flour). Add the milk and beat it through. Take ¾ of the berries and mash them with potato masher and toss them into the mixing bowl. Then add final quarter of berries whole. Grease a muffin tin and fill with batter. Sprinkle sugar over top and drop a little milk on top of each muffin. Bake 30 minutes at 375°. Let stand 30 minutes after removing from the oven. Eat instantly.

Watching
the Toast

William Stafford

When the toast gets darker and the burner turns off
a twilight comes. The whole world fades
toward now from Armageddon.

You could have been like the others—boastful,
cowardly, unfaithful, glowing like that,
but would be dull like this.

Outside in the early morning trees
move near: some of the things that happened
won't ever happen again.

Hungarian Potato Bread

Joy Williams

You need a 10-inch cast-iron fry pan and a cup of mashed potatoes. Boil the potatoes up ahead of time (save the water) or go out to dinner and order a baked potato instead of french fries (be sure to bring the potato home).

You need also:
1 package dry yeast
About 8 cups white
   unbleached flour
2½ cups warm water
2 tablespoons salt
1 tablespoon caraway seeds

Proof the yeast with ½ cup of the warm water and 3 tablespoons of flour for 30 minutes in a large bowl.

Add the remaining 2 cups of water, the salt and caraway seeds; then add the flour and the cup of mashed potatoes, and mix well. Turn out onto a floured board and knead for about 10 minutes. Shape the dough into a ball and put in an oiled bowl. Cover with a cloth, put in a warm spot, and let rise until doubled in bulk (about 2 hours).

Remove dough, punch down, knead for a few minutes, shape into a ball, and let rise in the greased fry pan for 30 minutes. Brush the loaf with water, sprinkle more caraway seeds on it, cut an X on it with a knife, and bake in a preheated 400° oven for 1 hour or even a little longer, until it is browned and sounds hollow when you rap on it, hello.

Peanut Butter Bread

Robley Wilson, Jr.

I'm not much of a cook, but during the ten months I was living in Canada to finish a novel, I did a lot of quick-bread baking, most especially a peanut butter bread. It goes like this:

2 cups flour
⅓ cup sugar
1 teaspoon salt
2 teaspoons baking powder
¾ cup peanut butter (Skippy or Kraft crunchy preferred)
1 egg
1 cup milk

Sift together the flour, sugar, salt, and baking powder. Use a fork to work the peanut butter and the egg into this dry mixture. Add the milk. Bake about 50 minutes in a 350° oven. (Oven temps vary, so start peeking at about 40 minutes.) The bread is much easier to slice when the loaf is cold (even chilled); on the other hand, it's delicious hot, and worth the crumbs.

* * *
SNACKS
AND
MISCELLANEOUS
* * *

The Great Paradise Lost Cheese Apple

Henri Coulette

When Adam and Eve took their solitary way (he in a crown of leaves, she in a fur coat), they took with them the first recipes, Snake Steak, Angel Soup.

Recipes are like poems; they keep what kept us. And good cooks are like good poets; they know how to count.

I have this recipe from my former wife. The apple is good the night of the party and the morning after.

8 ounces blue cheese
8 ounces smoky cheese
16 ounces cream cheese
1 tablespoon sour cream
4 tablespoons finely diced green
    pepper
4 tablespoons finely diced
    pimiento
Dash of garlic salt

Mix together; shape into apple; chill.

Coat with softened butter and cover with red-dyed, finely chopped almonds.

Serve with a fan of crackers and a knife.

Banana Sandwich

Stanley Elkin

I'm not much of a cook, more of an eater. And I don't really have any recipes but, if you'd like something I sometimes do make for myself and always enjoy, let it be the Banana Sandwich.

Slice a good ripe banana and place the chips on a Kaiser or other hard roll. A small dollop of mayonnaise may be added for lubricant, lettuce for texture. Sour cream makes an even better lubricant than mayonnaise. But in that case you can forget about your lettuce. A variant is to take an overripe banana and simply spread it like a kind of banana butter on your roll. I don't like the variant.

The Banana Sandwich must always be served with a tall cold glass of milk. Never with coffee, never with tea, or there's a curse.

Fried Mush

James Galvin

Follow the recipe on the back of the cornmeal box (always follow the recipe on the back of whatever package you're using), but add a little vanilla and an egg. After you've had whatever mush you want, let it set overnight. Then saw it up into slabs and fry it. You can put syrup on it.

Don't even try this recipe if there is anything else in the house to eat.

Although an experienced eater, my cooking tends toward the French Minimal in style. However, I can share with you

Herbert Gold's Early Lunch

(Especially tasty on mornings of revising final drafts)

Herbert Gold

1 slab Monterey Jack cheese
1 apple, chilled

Slice cheese in neat squares.
Slice apple in curved, organic hunks.
Staunch blood and bandage hand and serve.

This lunch, I have found, tends not to cause the dreaded Post-Lunch Drowsiness and Contentment with One's Lot. It also guarantees a tasty and satisfying dinner.

Bon Bon Chicken Sandwich

Barry Goldensohn

This requires good bread like a fresh baguette or seeded rye. Don't even bother if all you have is supermarket plastic wrap. The same for the peanut butter —-get a natural peanut butter, not Skippy's Hydrogenated Peanut Oil. Make a hot sauce out of it with your favorite mixture of peppers. I recommend Szechuan pepper, cayenne, and a dash of hot oil. Mix to taste. The rest is simple. Slap it on the bread with slices of peeled cucumber and leftover chicken (the moister the better).

The great virtue of this sandwich is that it is cheap, high calorie, and full of protein—very filling. It is also delicious. It should become part of that necessary body of knowledge of the world that is required to make chicken last for a week, and what other skill is more useful for setting the poets of America free from the bondage of lusting after money that keeps them from their proper work. I just wish one could build houses out of them, but the peanut butter takes too long to harden.

Black Bread, Butter, Onion, Coffee

Leonard Michaels

The black bread should be Pechter's, but the firm went out of business, so substitute bialys from the bakery on Grand Street, between Essex and Clinton, on the right side of the street heading toward the East River Drive, not Soho. With your thumbs, gouge, then tear the bialys open along the circumference. Butter the bialys. Insert onion slices. Do this around 3:00 A.M. at the glass-topped table in the dining room of my parents' apartment, after a heavy date in Greenwich Village. My parents should be asleep in their bedroom, about twenty feet away. Since my father is dead, imagine him. He snores. He cries out in his sleep against murderous assailants. I could never make out the exact words. Think what scares you most, then eat, eat. *The New York Times*, purchased half an hour ago, at the kiosk in Sheridan Square, is still fresh; it lies beside the plate of bialys. As you eat, read. Light a cigarette. Coffee, in the battered grey pot, waits on the stove. Don't let it boil. There should be occasional street noises—police sirens, yowling cats—penetrating the venetian blinds and thick, deeply pleated drapes of the living room windows. You feel the tender, powdery surface of the bialys dented by your fingertips which bear odors of sex. You also smell butter, bialy dough, onion, cigarette smoke, newsprint, and coffee. The whole city is in your nose. Still, you should go outside now, though it is after 3:00 A.M., and eat the last bialy while strolling down Cherry Street. The neighborhood is Mafia controlled; completely safe. You will be seen from tenement windows and recognized. Smoke another cigarette. Take your time. Your father cries out in his sleep, but he was born in Europe. As for you, a native American kid, there is nothing to worry about. Even if you eat half a dozen bialys, with an onion and two cups of coffee, you will sleep like a baby.

This is a recipe that I've been relying on most heavily this past fall.

Almost Infallible Cure for Writer's Block

Anne Tyler

1 jar Jif Extra-Crunchy peanut butter
1 jar strawberry jam, any brand that doesn't smush the berries too much

Dip a spoon into the peanut butter, then into the strawberry jam. Meditatively lick the mixture off the spoon. Repeat until you feel ready to go back to your workroom. (Usual dose: ¼ recipe)

This recipe comes from my highly pragmatic mother, who likes to have good food around for guests and doesn't like to spend a lot of time in the kitchen. I'd classify it as suburban cuisine, but it made enough of a hit with my graduate poetry class so they asked to have it run off with the poems on their final worksheet. It's rather colorful, like a Jackson Pollack painting, what with all the water chestnuts and vegetable bits from the powdered soup. And its especially delicious at about 2:00 A.M., when you're starving and have had the good sense not to lay in a supply of Swenson's French Vanilla and Hershey's Gold Brick Sauce. . . .

Spinach Dip

Leslie Ullman

2 packages chopped frozen
    spinach, cooked 1 minute
    and squeezed dry
1 can water chestnuts, chopped
    fine
1 cup mayonnaise
½ cup or more plain yogurt
    (you can use less mayo and
    more yogurt for less richness)
1 package Knorr's powdered
    vegetable soup (green and
    yellow box, usually available in
    supermarket gourmet sections)

Mix all together. It's best chilled several hours or overnight.

Strategies for Getting the Maximum Return for the Minimum Effort

Mary Carter

Asking *me* for a recipe is rather like asking Ronald Reagan to endorse the Communist Party—I hate to cook, and one of the many felicities of living alone is that I don't have to cook. I do however love to eat, so have developed strategies for getting the maximum return for the minimum effort. I'm happiest when my diet, like my life, is stripped back to fundamentals: fruit, vegetables, nuts, yogurt, chicken, and fish. This may appear symptomatic of an elaborately advanced—or regressive, depending on your politics—lifestyle; it is, in fact, simply my individual biological imperative. I mean, I *could* be living the CuisinArt, stir-fry philosophy, but that would be a patent sham.

I love to grow vegetables—spade the soil and plant them and water them and weed them and brood over them and pick them—as well as to eat them, and if I ever get settled again that's what I'll do. From this one would infer that I yearn to grow and trample my own grapes for wine (not so, as long as I can buy Folonari Soave) and knead my own bread (vehemently not so. I would rather handle a snake. The one time I tried kneading bread it came alive and crept up my arms, and if I hadn't yelled for help it would have engulfed and strangled me). But there's not enough substance to store-bought bread—substance, heft, and clout is the point of bread—so I developed a recipe, or strategy rather (all my "recipes" are really strategies).

For 2 regular-size loaves, one of which you have to freeze and the other refrigerate (it won't keep; and nobody else is going to help you eat it, not even your best friend): heat the oven to 350° and spray inside the loaf pans with Pam. In a large bowl mix the dry ingredients: 4 cups whole wheat flour, 4 cups unprocessed bran (some of this can be soy flour, oatmeal, wheat germ, cornmeal), 2 tablespoons baking powder, 2 cups dry milk solids, salt (if you must; I prefer to *infer* the salt, a form of sensory deprivation that is its own reward). In a smaller bowl mix the liquids: ¾ cup oil, 3 large eggs (or ¾ cup Eggbeaters, if you worry about cholesterol), and 5 cups water (or whey, from dripping your too-thin yogurt in a cheesecloth bag to yield yogurt "cheese"). Pour the liquids all at once into the dry mixture, stir (but don't beat) to mix, pour into pans, bake for 60–90 minutes. What you have, of course, is two enormous bran muffins, without the sugar (which you can add, if you insist). If you dropped one on your foot, you would never again be able to enter a marathon. You toast fairly thick slices—not in a toaster; it's too crumbly. Use a portable or oven broiler—and have them for breakfast: spread not with butter but with English marmalade and atop that your yogurt "cheese." If you can stand the excitement, you can live on this indefinitely.

Other strategies (for people who genuinely eschew cooking):

For fish: it is urgent to live where bluefish are available—Martha's Vineyard, for instance (rosemary bushes are all very well, but bluefish is bliss). You get the largest chunk of the largest piece, put it skinside down on your broiler. Assemble (and apply, in this order) lemon juice, a goodly spread of yogurt, garlic powder, a little salt and pepper. Broil just until the flesh becomes opaque. You will probably pig out and eat it all the first night—a friend will be all too delighted to help you—so you'll have to do it all over again the next night, and the next, as long as the bluefish are running. People will wonder why it tastes so great, and you will have to admit that it is the garlic.

If you have a garden, you will have more tomatoes and zucchini than you know what to do with. Do not give these away to your friends. Live on tomatoes, zucchini, and giant bran muffins. With the tomatoes you have to sow a couple rows of large-leaf sweet basil, which you chop up (breaking the no-chop rule) and mix with sliced tomatoes, Italian style. Also Italian style, you take the male squash blossoms and either use them in a salad, or dip them in egg batter and sauté them in olive oil for a sort of fritatta. You can make a fritatta from the zucchini too.

For a class act with reverse definition (the art of making the easy look difficult) try as an hors d'oeuvre, or as the first course of a summer supper party, Smoked Salmon Mousse:

Soften an envelope of unflavored gelatin over 3 tablespoons lemon juice and 3 tablespoons scotch. Then dissolve it, stirring constantly, over simmering water; set aside, but not too long. Combine in blender: a 15½-ounce can red salmon (the pink is cheaper but it looks gray; make a batch of *that* for yourself, putting it into 8-ounce yogurt cartons to take to the office for your paper-bag lunches), ½ cup mayonnaise, 1 cup yogurt, and ¼ teaspoon Liquid Smoke. Add the dissolved gelatin and blend thoroughly (you may have to flake the salmon in gradually). Pour it into an oiled or Pam'd 5-cup mold or small casserole and chill for a couple hours. (You can put a pinch of salt in this if you want, but I don't). If youre using it as an hors d'oeuvre, mold it in a wild, shallow soup bowl—or two, or three—and serve with crackers.

Finally: you buy a crock pot, chuck meat, and vegetables in in the morning, and when you totter home from work there's dinner. Turkey thighs are good this way, and the broth's great. Stew cut-up lemon chunks—peels and all—with this and eat with other veg's.

Here is my entire repertoire of recipes, two. They are close to my heart.

Marinade

Don Hendrie Jr.

I cannot, do not, and will not cook. I do, however, wish to pass on a certain marinade which will turn top round into the finest sirloin, and beyond. My father is the inventor.

¼ cup soy oil
¼ cup good bourbon
1 sliced garlic bud
2 teaspoons soy sauce
1 teaspoon Worcestershire sauce
Freshly ground pepper
1 teaspoon freshly ground ginger root
1 tablespoon brown sugar

Whisk these ingredients together and pour over your cut of beef. Turn the beef every hour or so for an entire day. Before cooking, dry off with paper towels. Toss the marinade. Broil the beef.

Survivor's Cottage Cheese

Since 1964 I have been enamored of what I shall call "Survivor's Cottage Cheese." To a bowl of large curd cottage cheese add: a dollop of mayonnaise, freshly ground pepper, diced bread-and-butter pickles (preferably Mrs. Fannin's, from Best Foods), a tablespoon of sweet corn relish, and—most important—the juice and meat of 5 vine-ripened cherry tomatoes. Mix thoroughly and serve with a handful of absolutely fresh saltines. The concoction may also be served on saltines as an hors d'oeuvre. The Ultimate Fussy Lunch.

Keeley

Edmund Keeley

As a writer, the only recipes I have anything to do with are alcoholic. I offer one that has become mildly famous in Princeton as a poor man's version of the Italian's Negroni, diminished to something closer to an Americano. It is called, in these regions, a Keeley, and it consists of equal parts of gin and Campari, to which you add either soda, tonic, or Bitter Lemon (depending on the range of your sweet tooth; I prefer tonic), and in any case several slices of fresh lime.

Blake's No-Cook Barbecue Sauce

Constance Urdang

It feels oddly appropriate to me to be sending this recipe for the Writers' Workshop cookbook since it was given to me by a fellow-worker in the University Hospitals when I was writing poems in the Workshop and moonlighting to keep body and soul together.

41

1 cup sugar
½ teaspoon salt
¼ teaspoon pepper
1 teaspoon dry mustard
1 tablespoon celery seed
¾ cup vinegar
½ cup oil
1 can tomato sauce
1 medium onion, grated
1 close garlic, minced
Dash of Worcestershire sauce

Mix all dry ingredients together. Add vinegar; then oil; then tomato sauce. Beat to mix. Then add onion, garlic, Worcestershire sauce. Stir. Pour into 2 pint jars and refrigerate.

This is wonderful on chicken, ribs, or hamburgers. It can also be used as a salad dressing.

This recipe is called

Eggs on Horseback,

or Oeufs au Cheval.

Robert Anderson

Cut the crusts off slices of bread. . . . Separate white from yolks, keeping yolks *unbroken* (a neat trick). . . . Whip up the whites till firm. . . . Put slice of cheese or grated cheese on piece of bread. . . . Spread thickened whites of eggs over bread and cheese and make slight indentation in stiff whites. Slip unbroken egg yolk into this indentation. Put slices of bread on pastry sheet and bake.

Carry Rivers's Cheese Soufflé

Gail Godwin

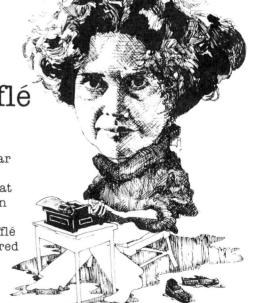

Since I was served this a year ago at a dinner party in Washington, I have made it at least a dozen times for my own guests. It always comes out right, and it is the only soufflé I know of that can be prepared the night before.

10 slices (or more) day-old white bread: cut off crusts
    and cut into triangles
1 pound sharp Cheddar cheese, grated
4 whole eggs, beaten
2½ cups milk
1 tablespoon grated onion
½ teaspoon Worcestershire sauce
½ teaspoon dry mustard
1 teaspoon salt
Pinch of cayenne, or shake of Tabasco
Paprika

Grease bowl. Layer bread (first) and cheese to top of bowl. Combine eggs, milk, and seasonings. Pour over top. Sprinkle with paprika.

Stand in refrigerator at least 3 hours, or overnight. Bake for one hour at 350°. (I put it in when the guests come up the driveway. That gives an hour for drinks, etc.) It can be served as a main dish for four, with salad as a light meal. For a more substantial meal—or for larger number of guests— serve it as a side dish with an entree of chicken or ham.

The High-Cholesterol Breakfast

John Hawkes

A 12-inch skillet
3 eggs
3 poaching rings
3 slices country bacon, ⅛ inch
    in thickness
¼ pound country sausage
English muffins
French coffee

My tastes ordinarily run to French cooking. However, once a week, on Sunday morning, I indulge a sudden urge toward a genuine American meal and toward subverting all we know about healthful eating. Hence this special breakfast, the main ingredient of which is what I call "cowboy eggs," or eggs cooked in deep fat. The process is obvious: fry the meat in the skillet, being sure not to overcook the bacon, which should turn a mere golden translucency with the lean portions invitingly red.. Remove the meat from the skillet, leaving *all* of the bacon and sausage fat in the pan. (There should be ½ to ¼ inch of fat in the pan.) Place the poaching rings in the pan, break the eggs into the rings. Fry the eggs until the yolks are the color of a blood orange, *basting constantly with the fat.*

There's no breakfast more richly American than this one, set off handsomely by the French coffee. And for anyone with a rebellious and possibly self-destructive nature, it goes as far as possible toward breaking the cholesterol taboo.

Eggs Maledict

Howard Nemerov

Instead of English muffins,
    Wonder Bread
Instead of ham, Spam
Instead of hollandaise,
    Kraft mayonnaise
Eggs fried instead of coddled

Soufflé

Grace Paley

Combine 1 container ricotta cheese with ½ container cottage cheese. Beat 2 eggs into it and some grated cheese.

Add 1 package of frozen spinach or its equivalent in fresh spinach that has been cooked and get all the water out.

Mix together and bake at 350° until done. If you sautée onions and mushrooms and add them to the mixture before baking, it gives it a really nice taste.

Soft-Boiled Eggs

Reynolds Price

An egg is the most elegantly packaged of natural foods, and too few Americans consume it directly from its beautiful container. The pleasure of that transaction can, however, come only after the acquisition of skill in soft-boiling. Twenty-four years of practice have perfected the following method.

Remove a cold fresh egg from storage (if your egg is at room temperature, do not use this method). Set it in a small saucepan and add just enough cold water to cover. Set the pan on a cold electric eye and bring to a rapid boil. Begin timing from the moment of full boil. Be serious. I use a stop watch. Ten extra seconds and you'll be in trouble. A supermarket extra-large egg will soft-boil in precisely four minutes. Remove promptly from the heat, pour off hot water, douse the egg with cold water, and set it in an attractive or humorous eggcup. Decapitate, three-quarters of an inch below the peak of the smaller end, with a smart rap from the blade of a dull knife. Proceed to eat directly from the shell, with whatever accompaniments facilitate your waking. I choose salt and pepper, a slice of whole grain bread with salt-free margarine, a little jam, and strong coffee. Another day launched, neatly and skillfully.

Recipe for Sunday Morning (sans cockatoos)

Michael Ryan

One sufficiently fat liberal
   bourgeois newspaper.
Three hours of sufficiently
   familiar baroque music.
Plenty of sunlight (difficult to
   obtain in Iowa, in winter).
6 eggs
1 teaspoon butter
Grated Parmesan cheese (must
   be fresh)
Mushrooms
Freshly ground pepper in
   abundance
A little salt
Herbs, with discretion
Whatever else is in the
   refrigerator

Melt the butter in a frying pan. Sauté the mushrooms (green peppers, shallots) for a moment. Take the pan off the heat and break into the eggs, grate into it the Parmesan, salt, pepper, herbs (basil and parsley are particularly good), etc. Bacon, ham, salami optional. When it's all there, inert, break the yolks with a big spoon, stir (in sprung rhythm), return the pan to low heat, and continue stirring (I caught this morning morning's minion, I caught this morning morning's minion) until the eggs are of the consistency you like. Eat them with a friend. Be complacent about the accomplishment of Western culture in a decadent period of history. Serve with fresh sliced tomatoes.

The recipe is infinitely variable. You can, for example, sauté a few pieces of apple in the butter, add the eggs and a touch of honey.

It isn't our fault, is it?

For those who nearly like Eggs Benedict, but find the preparation of the sauce too time-consuming and the dish itself a little too rich for the palate and too elegant for their spirits, here's a breakfast the folks hereabouts call Egg McMiller. I, being a modest sort, call it

Eggs Fayetteville

Miller Williams

4 eggs
2 English muffins
Block of Monterey Jack cheese
Small can of tomato sauce
Hot taco sauce (optional)
Sausage for patties
Salt

Skillet
Large saucepan with lid
Small saucepan
Long-handled frictionless (Teflon or other plastic or smooth
    wood) perforated dipper or large-bowl spoon
Soup bowl

Preheat the oven to 400(Slice the 2 muffins and cover each
of the 4 halves with a thick slice of cheese (I suggest Monterey
Jack because it melts with the right consistency for this
dish). Place them in the oven on a cookie sheet for 8 minutes
or until the cheese is melted. Remove and place on warmer.

Pour the tomato sauce into the small saucepan (add up to
a tablespoon of taco sauce if your taste runs to hotter foods)
and bring to a simmer. Remove and place on warmer.

Fry 4 sausage patties and place on warmer.

The eggs are poached *in camicia:* Break the eggs into the
soup bowl, taking care not to break the yolks. Bring to boil
in the large saucepan about 2½ inches of water to which has
been added ⅛ teaspoon of salt. Slide the eggs gently into the
boiling water, cover the saucepan, and turn off the heat.

After 7 or 8 minutes (less time for fewer eggs; the exact
time will vary with the size of the eggs, the elevation, the
hardness of the water, the thickness of the saucepan, the fit
of the lid and one's preference for harder or softer poached
eggs) remove the eggs with the dipper and slide one each
onto the prepared half muffins. Pour 2 tablespoons of sauce
over each egg and serve with a sausage pattie on the side.

It's not difficult to time the frying of the sausage, the
poaching of the eggs, and the melting of the cheese so that
everything comes out pretty much together. The sauce can
be heated in a couple of minutes at any point in the process.

Heavy eaters will take 2 of everything; most will want 1
egg dish and 1 pattie, so the recipe as given here serves 2 to 4.

When this is served as a mid- or late-morning breakfast,
it's very nice to prepare the way for it with a drink I call O.
Jordan (for orange juice and the woman I wake up with it).
For each drink: Into a large wine glass place a tablespoon of
frozen orange juice, thawed until mushy. Pour chilled white
wine over this until the glass is ½ to ⅔ full and top with a
good chilled soda water. Stir well, until the orange pulp is
barely dissolved and a slight foam forms on the mixture. Serve
at once.

Onward.

* * *

PASTA

* * *

Bob and Peg Dana's Fettucine with Black Olive Sauce

Robert Dana

When I was visiting poet at the University of Florida, Peg and I began a romance with pasta.

One of my advanced poetry-writing students was an associate professor of mathematics, now longtime friend, James Brooks. Jim was passionate not only about books, poetry, and all the other things attendant on the art, he was also passionate about homemade pasta. "The sauce?" he would say, "The hell with the sauce. The sauce is just an excuse to eat the pasta. You don't even need a sauce. Just some butter and cheese." Nevertheless, he could also be ardent about sauces.

It was in Jim and Gretchen's kitchen that I was persuaded to put my hands directly into a bowl of eggs and flour, to peel and seed tomatoes, and learned to cook pasta *al dente*.

The Greek olives in this sauce (I sometimes use the big Syrian ones if Calamatas aren't available) are an innovation of my own. I think I began using them when I was visiting poet at Wayne State University in Detroit because the Eastern market there provided a ready supply. Or perhaps it was only then that I began to make black olive sauce regularly. (American olives are canned in water and thus have a taste akin to high-grade cardboard, nothing approaching real Mediterranean olives.)

In any case, this recipe has become a staple of Dana family

cuisine. A no-fail specialty. And what mathematical formula or poetic theory can rival that?

Fettucine *(If you make your own)*

1¼ cups white flour
1 whole egg
3 egg yolks
1 teaspoon olive oil (preferably a light Spanish oil)
1–2 teaspoons salt

This quantity of ingredients will make about ¾ pound of pasta. We usually figure a minimum of 4 ounces of pasta per person for an average dinner, so make 2 batches.

Fill a pasta kettle with plenty of water, liberally salted. Bring to a furious boil. Add pasta. If fresh, begin tasting after 2 or 3 minutes. If dried pasta, after 4 minutes. If commercial pasta, after 6 or 7 minutes. Stop cooking when it's still chewy or *al dente*. Pasta shouldn't be soft and overcooked. Drain immediately in a colander or sieve. Do not blanch under cold water.

Crush a clove of garlic with a teaspoon and rub the inside of a pasta dish. When the pasta has sufficiently drained, toss pasta in the dish with a little olive oil before topping with sauce.

Black Olive Sauce *(for 4)*

2 medium onions, sliced in rings
4 medium to large tomatoes
16–20 Greek olives
Salt and pepper
Olive oil

Sauté onion rings over low heat until translucent. Use a splash of olive oil, sufficient to coat the bottom of the skillet.

Submerge tomatoes for less than 1 minute in just-boiled water. Skin under cold water, remove seeds, cut into wedges, and add to onions. (Home-canned tomatoes may be used if seeded and well drained.)

Add olives whole or with pits removed, salt, and pepper. Simmer 10 minutes or less. Drain off excess juice and top pasta with the sauce.

Grated cheese

Grate a sufficient quantity of fresh Romano or Parmesan into a bowl and let your guests help themselves. Avoid commercial sawdusts.

Bread

If a good Italian bread isn't available, a sourdough, or hard-crusted roll will serve.

Wine

A good chianti is always a fine accompaniment. Look for the black rooster on the neck label.

Commuter's Pasta

Gwen Head

I live in Seattle, and do most of my writing there. But I also work at Dragon Gate, Inc., which publishes books out of offices in a Victorian house in Port Townsend, Washington,

a mere thirty miles away "as the crow flies." The crow doesn't
fly, however; instead the hapless commuter (me) is faced
with several possible combinations of charming but
inefficient ferries, and roads whose design strongly supports
a belief in the existence of sasquatches, at least in the
Highway Department. The whole complex land-and-water
passage takes a minimum of three hours, under those ideal
conditions that never seem to exist. Once here, or there, the
commuting poet-editor (me) is confronted with an
immutable law. Since it seems to involve such perverse and
inexplicable phenomena as the apparent teleportation of a
wide variety of objects, let's call it Yuri Geller's Law: Whatever
you want to work on, read, wear, eat, or drink is always on
the other end of the line. The inexorable operation of Geller's
Law, however, can be an incentive, if not to real "creativity"
at least to that spirit of lively improvisation in the face of an
odd or exigent selection of possible ingredients that is at the
heart of classic cuisine. As in a favorite recipe from the
Larousse Gastronomique that begins "Take two ducks and
four bottles of Gevrey Chambertin . . ." Or in the following
humble recipe for "Commuter's Pasta," conceived on an
evening of exceptionally late arrival, when my other culinary
options were starvation or dinner at a local restaurant
renowned for its antique fish. (There are some quite
wonderful restaurants in Port Townsend. They all close at
nine. They vacuum your toes to remind you.) My kitchen
cupboards contained coffee, rice, a can of olives,* another can
of bean soup, a loaf of bread ready to be declared a National
Mold Sanctuary, a can of American (or fake) Parmesan
cheese, and half of a one-pound box of spinach pasta.* In the
refrigerator, aside from an unopened bottle of champagne*
left over from a friend's wedding reception, I found nothing
but several heads of garlic* and a large lemon*; in the freezer
were two rigid bait herring, one-third of a wedding cake
swathed in a green plastic garbage bag, and a package of
precooked breakfast sausage.* Here is how to coax the most
promising of these ingredients into a convincing semblance
of edibility. NOTE: it is most important that the *unstarred*
ingredients listed above be omitted, as their inclusion, in
whole or in part, could be deadly. For more gregarious
commuters I have adapted the recipe to serve four.

1 8-ounce box spinach pasta
1 8-ounce box frozen precooked breakfast sausage, sliced

1 3½-ounce can large black olives, sliced
¼ cup Parmesan cheese
3 large cloves garlic
Juice of 1 large lemon
Boiling salted water

Optional but highly desirable:

¼–½ cup heavy cream
Friends who leave champagne in your refrigerator

Brown the sliced breakfast sausage over moderate heat, adding finely minced garlic when the sausage is about half done. Pour off the sausage grease; add the juice of ¾ of the lemon and the sliced olives. Stir thoroughly and let all the ingredients simmer, covered, over the lowest possible heat, for a minute or two. In the meantime you have of course had the foresight to boil the spinach noodles, which are now precisely *al dente.* Now drain them *very* thoroughly, return to the hot cooking pot, and toss with the sausage, olive and garlic mixture, and the Parmesan cheese. Add the juice of the remaining ¼ lemon, or more as needed; the mixture should be pleasantly tangy, with enough lemon to balance the heaviness of the sausage, olive and cheese flavors. If you have heavy cream, add some; the cheese will melt into it, making a light, delectable sauce. This recipe would be even better, of course, with imported Parmesan, Romano, or Pecorino cheese, homemade spinach pasta, and any good mild, but above all unfrozen sausage. But at least you have the champagne to console you.

Pasta Sauce with Shrimp

John Irving

I don't have a lot of recipes. I mean, I don't write them down. Here's the best sauce for pasta (angel hair or fettucine—that range) I've happened upon recently.

Crisp 2 or more strips of bacon in an iron skillet or heavy-bottomed saucepan.

Remove bacon and drain; remove all but 2 tablespoons of the bacon fat from the skillet. Add 1 tablespoon of olive oil, 2 generous handfuls of *good olives—it doesn't matter if they're pitted or not.* Make sure the oil is hot when you add the olives.

Immediately, into the hot oil, add some fresh shrimp—split up the back and deveined, but still in their shells. The shells are important because half the shrimp's flavor is in the shell. Turn the shrimp until they're pink on both sides and the shells are even beginning to crisp and brown (but not burn).

Remove the shrimp from the hot oil; put them on a plate but *don't* drain them, because the oil that's on them should eventually be returned to the sauce.

Into the hot oil (not much of it, and it's okay to add another tablespoon of olive oil—just get it hot) put a handful of fresh basil; when it wilts, add 6 or 7 ripe tomatoes, quartered (depending on how many shrimp you have; you might use 2 handfuls of basil and 12 tomatoes). Mash the tomatoes down in the oil and simmer the basil and tomatoes with the olives for about 10 to 15 minutes or until the tomatoes are very soft and dissolving.

Strain the sauce through a food mill and return to the pan. If the olives are pitted, they'll strain through easily; if they're not, just pick them out and simmer the sauce another 10 minutes; check seasoning with salt and pepper.

When you serve it over pasta, sprinkle the crumbled bacon and some fresh parsley on top—Parmesan isn't so great with a fish or shellfish sauce, not even in a tomato-based sauce, but some people like it anyway.

Pasta Boccaccio

Robie Macauley

8 ounces Gorgonzola cheese
½ cup milk
6 tablespoons butter
Dash salt
Dash white pepper

Mash cheese in a large skillet. Add milk, butter, salt and pepper and simmer gently on low heat until mixture is creamy.

½ cup light cream
1 egg yolk

Mix egg yolk with cream and add some of the hot liquid before adding the cream to the skillet.

½ cup Parmesan cheese

Stir into the above. Simmer gently. A dash of brandy can be added at this time.

¾–1 pound cooked pasta
   (linguine or tagliolini)

Add pasta to the sauce and stir until coated with sauce and warm.

Serve with salad and crusty Italian bread.

Many years ago, in a far-off town called New Haven, Connecticut, I worked in an Italian restaurant called "Frankie's." I learned there a skill? a craft? an art? which has provided me with much comfort ever since. Being a Celt and not entirely happy until I had adapted "Roman" style to my own needs, I developed the following recipe. It can be cooked in say 20 minutes and will provide a substantial and delectable meal in a hurry. (I have some sort of Jungian notion in my racial unconscious that the Celts always ate on the move. I almost said "on the run," but that would be too IRA.)

Spaghetti Irlandese

William Murray

Spaghetti in boiling water to which salt and a few drops of olive oil have been added.

Small white onion sliced and dropped in boiling water with spaghetti.

Add mixed green vegetables straight from frozen package (broccoli, chopped spinach, celery).

About 5 minutes before *al dente,* add frozen shrimp.

When the spaghetti is done, strain the whole mess through a colander and rinse briefly in cold water.

Empty onto large *warm* platter. Add butter and egg yolk.

Use a pinch of garlic salt if you want flavor.

White wine natch, for a delicate Celtic recipe
like this. It is not Mrs. Murphy's chowder.

Pasta Primavera
(for two or three)

Stanley Plumly

1 pound fresh spaghetti (a little
   eggy if possible)
A couple of carrots, thinly
   sliced)
1 zucchini, thinly sliced
1 small yellow onion, sliced
Some Italian seasoning,
   including the following—
   marjoram, thyme, rosemary,
   savory, sage, oregano (fresh
   if possible; all minced and
   mixed)
Fresh basil, minced
A little parsley
¼ pound or so of butter
4–5 full-size peeled Italian
   tomatoes
A bit of Romano cheese
A tad of Parmesan cheese
Salt and pepper to taste

    1. Sauté the sliced onion in the butter.
    2. Add the vegetables, including tomatoes, and bring to a
bit of a boil.
    3. Add seasoning (except basil) and simmer for a while;
then add basil and Romano cheese.
    4. Cook pasta according to directions.
    5. Drain pasta and place on plates.
    6. Add sauce, with Parmesan cheese and a little parsley.
    I probably forgot something. I do it out of my head each
time, so it comes out a little original, always.

Spaghetti Carbonara

Mark Strand

2–3 large eggs
⅓ cup freshly grated Parmesan
cheese
⅓ pound bacon
1 pound spaghetti
1 medium onion, roughly
chopped
½ cup prosciutto, ¹/₁₆-inch
slices, roughly chopped
⅓ cup heavy cream
3 tablespoons chopped parsley
½ teaspoon salt
Freshly ground pepper

1. Heat 6 quarts of water with 2 tablespoons of olive oil and 1 tablespoon of salt. Proceed while the water is coming to a boil.

2. Beat the eggs in a large bowl and stir in the Parmesan cheese. Set aside.

3. Cook the bacon in a large skillet until all the fat is rendered but it is not altogether crisp. Remove the bacon with a slotted spoon and drain it on paper towels. Also drain off some of the bacon fat. When the bacon has cooled, crumble it into small pieces and set aside.

4. Cook the pasta in boiling water until *al dente*. Strain the pasta in a colander thoroughly and quickly.

5. While the pasta is cooking, cook the onions in the bacon fat over moderate heat until soft, about 5 minutes. Add the prosciutto and stir.

6. As soon as the pasta is drained, transfer it to the large skillet. Pour the egg and cheese mixture into skillet. Toss until the strands are coated. Add the heavy cream, parsley,

salt, and pepper. Toss again and serve with additional grated Parmesan cheese on the side.

Serves 4–6

NOTE: If prosciutto is unavailable, substitute smoked ham or Canadian bacon (cooking the Canadian bacon for a few minutes with the onions), or ¼ pound of salt pork, diced small and sautéed until the fat is rendered.

My Husband's Favorite Macaroni and Cheese Dish

Mona Van Duyn

My husband, Jarvis Thurston, asks for this dish at least once a month, and I am glad to oblige, since it couldn't be easier.

1 7-ounce package of macaroni
¾ pound Cheddar or sharp
   Cheddar
1 8-ounce carton fresh
   mushrooms
1 1-pound can whole tomatoes
1 medium onion
1½ cups milk
Salt and pepper
A 3-quart casserole

Boil and drain macaroni. Mix half the macaroni with the onion, which has been chopped, in the bottom of the casserole. Distribute half the cheese, which has been cut into chunks approximately 1 inch by 1 inch by ½ inch on top. Spread the mushrooms, thickly sliced, over this. Cut tomatoes in half and distribute on top of mushrooms, adding the juice in the can. Add rest of macaroni. Salt and pepper to taste. Distribute the rest of the cheese chunks on top, pour the milk over all. Bake, uncovered, for 1 hour in a 375° oven.

Pasta Sauce

Arturo Vivante

Alas I'm not a good cook. My way of making a sauce for pasta is to simmer some tomato paste and half a cup of water in olive oil for a *long* time, till there are a few flecks of carbon, then mixing it into the pasta right away, lest the spaghetti or whatever stick together.

* * *

VEGETARIAN MAIN DISHES

* * *

Conroy's All-Purpose Dhal

Frank Conroy

Very inexpensive and highly nutritious. Full of protein for impoverished artists. It is so delicious I continue to make it even though I am now rich. In the top of a double boiler, heat ¼ cup vegetable oil. Add ½ cup chopped onion. Garlic if you like. Cook until wilted, add 1 cup *red* lentils. Stir for 3 or 4 minutes over a moderate flame.

Add 2 cups of water and 2 chicken bouillon cubes. Add a stick of cinnamon, the juice of half a lime, and the squeezed half-lime itself. Now put the top of the double boiler onto the bottom, and cook for about an hour and a half. That is the basic sauce, and is excellent as is.

However, you can add at this point: 1) ½ cup onions sautéed in ¼ cup oil or butter; 2) sautéed red peppers in same; 3) curry powder; 4) sesame oil; 5) chili powder; and 6) leftover meat or anything else you think might make it interesting.

This Dhal is terrific. Maggie and I eat it most often with rice, but we have enjoyed it as a spaghetti sauce, or on bread (like peanut butter), or as a dip, after readings.

Black-eyed Peas Creole

Andre Dubus

Today is the anniversary of the death of Chekhov and Hemingway. My wife and three-week-old daughter and I went to the beach. The girl has red hair, is lovely, and is named Cadence Yvonne.

1 pound black-eyed peas
  (beans)
1 clove garlic
2 stalks celery
1 onion
1 ham hock

Soak beans overnight, then drain and cover with about 3 inches of water. Add ham hock. In skillet, sauté in butter or vegetable oil, garlic clove, finely choped, celery stalks, chopped, onion, chopped. When they soften, add them to the beans. Bring beans to a boil, fairly cover with black pepper, then simmer on low until they are tender (about 2 hours).

The recipe can also be used for red beans, adding a chopped bell pepper to the skillet to sauté with onions, celery, and garlic. The black-eyed pea wants gentle seasoning, but the red bean can take more. I often add a chopped jalapeño pepper, seeds and all, to the pot of beans. Also, with red beans, you can experiment: I sometimes add a tablespoon of honey or brown sugar or molasses to every hot ingredient. (One jalepeño to the spoon of honey; cayenne pepper and sugar; and molasses.) And, because of the strength of the red bean, you can add your favorite sausages to the pot, as soon as you start to cook the beans.

Both of these are good as leftovers, cold as a salad with sliced onions, oil and vinegar; or fried with leftover rice in a skillet.

Both are normally served over rice, which, according to *The Times Picayune Creole Cook Book* of 1901, should be cooked like this: Bring 1 quart of water, with a teaspoon of salt, to boil. Wash a cup of rice in cold water. Add rice to briskly boiling water, stirring occasionally, but *only* until the grains thicken. Then *do not stir* again. The boiling water will keep the rice from sticking. Boil until grains are soft, about 25 minutes. Then drain the water and put, uncovered, in the oven, where the rice will dry. It will then be soft, and should be put immediately into a bowl.

I do not cook beans with salt, because of salt's disfavor; the ham hock and pepper work well, and of course people can salt their own servings. If you wish to cook with salt, a teaspoon is enough.

I have chosen these recipes because they have been consistently popular with New England friends. They are always inexpensive, and they refrigerate or freeze well. In one bleak financial year, while living alone, I often cooked a pound of beans on the weekend, and had hearty sustenance for days, for the price of a six-pack.

Cottage Cheese Enchiladas

Nicholas Meyer
(Alex. Dumas I ain't)

Someone once taught me to make something called *Cottage Cheese Enchiladas*. The good news about this dish is that it tastes great but is considerably less fattening than regular enchiladas. You'll need:

Flour or corn tortillas
Oil
Cottage cheese
Sliced olives
Scallions, sliced
Enchilada sauce
American cheese or somesuch

First you mix the cottage cheese together with your supply of sliced scallions and sliced olives—the more of these little guys the tastier everything's gonna be.

Then you lightly soak your tortilla in hot oil (use a frying pan). Use a paper towel to soak up the excess oil on the tortilla.

Then you roll a tortilla—full of your cottage cheese/olive/scallion combo and put it in a baking pan. (Not too thick!)

When you've got as many tortillas as you want, you open the enchilada sauce and pour it over all of them. Then you grate some cheese (I usually use American, but any kind will work) over the whole thing and stick it in the oven. By the time your grated cheese has melted it's probably ready to serve.

This recipe is in memory of Sarkis Renjilian, the old Armenian, who cooked this pilaf for me many times, who gave me a taste for Arak, the liquor that makes you hold your tongue, for garlic, for beautiful rugs in a room that let in no light, and allowed me, begrudgingly I think, the company of his four lovely daughters, when I was a teen-ager.

Renjilian Pilaf

Steve Orlen

1½ cups brown rice
Enough small egg noodles to lightly cover the bottom of a
   large frying pan
Light vegetable cooking oil
Liberal amounts of cumin,
   paprika, and allspice
3 cups bouillon

Brown the uncooked egg noodles in oil, being careful not to burn, and turning frequently. Add remainder of ingredients and simmer 45 minutes or until the rice is done. If desired, add chopped lamb, or spinach, or raisins, before cooking. Eat only in the kitchen.

David's Enchiladas

Maura Stanton

I eat these enchiladas twice a week, and if I"m feeling in any way depressed I get over it right away. The recipe comes from David Wojahn. One summer in late June my husband, Richard Cecil, and I came back from five weeks in Greece. It was 105° in Tucson and we knew we faced a whole long summer of such heat or worse. (It was still 101° on October 1 that year!) We felt trapped inside our house by the heat—the only place to walk was the air-conditioned shopping mall. Then David Wojahn and Julie Fay invited us to dinner. As I ate David's enchiladas and Julie's guacamole, and listened to the hum of the swamp cooler and the rasp of the cicadas outside, which sounded just like the cicadas in Greece, I felt much better. David's enchiladas have never failed to cheer me up, even if I thought I was cheerful to begin with. Here's his simple recipe: Soften flour tortillas, one at a time, in oil and butter in a skillet. Place a tablespoon or so each of grated Cheddar cheese, chopped olives, chopped onions, and a spoonful of enchilada sauce near the edge of each tortilla, roll up, and tuck in the ends. Place in a casserole dish or pie pan and pour most of the enchilada sauce (1 10-ounce can for every 6 tortillas will do) over all. Bake in a

350° oven for 25 minutes. Add the rest of the sauce (to keep the tortillas from getting dry) and bake for 5 minutes more. Eat with refried beans and/or guacamole. Drink Dos Equis or club soda with lime.

Tofu Tempura

Mary Swander

Cut tofu in small chunks; pierce holes in it with a fork.

Combine ½ cup whole wheat flour, ½ teaspoon baking powder, ½ cup cornstarch, ½ teaspoon salt, and 1 cup water. Mix until smooth. Dip tofu in this mixture and fry in deep, hot oil.

Curried Rice

Thom Swiss

In the early months of my wife's pregnancy, Cynthia developed a taste for spicy foods, especially Indian, Tai, and Mexican dishes. As it happened, she was teaching in the early evening, which meant the cooking would be my job for the year.

I'm not a very good cook—I lack the patience—but I took my new job seriously and sought out the advice of friends as well as a variety of books.

Curried rice is a side dish. This particular recipe is easy to make, and—if I might say this without sounding like I"m selling a cookbook—it's a colorful dish. I usually make it with a main course that is lightly seasoned—something like broiled whitefish or spinach soufflé.

1½ cups brown rice
4 cups water
¾ teaspoon salt
2 tablespoons olive oil
¼ cup chopped onion
1 clove garlic, slivered
½ cup chopped green pepper
½ cup sunflower seeds
¼ teaspoon curry powder
½ cup raisins
¼ teaspoon curry powder

Add the rice to 3 cups of boiling salted water. Bring to a boil again, let boil for 2 minutes, then reduce heat and simmer, covered, about 50 minutes. While the rice is cooking, place a frying pan over medium heat and add the oil. When the oil is hot, add the onion and garlic and stir for several minutes. Add the green pepper, sunflower seeds, and curry. Stir for another few minutes. Add the raisins and the remaining cup of water, reduce heat, and simmer with lid ajar for 10 minutes or so until liquid is half gone. Combine curry mixture with rice about 15 minutes before rice is done. Be careful to mix gently so that the rice stays fluffy. Cook together without additional stirring until done, mix lightly, and serve. Makes 4 servings.

* * *

BEEF

* * *

Mongolian Hot-Pot

Stephen Becker

This recipe is anathema to vegetarians and cholesterophobes, but to us Mongolian nomads, after a hard day riding the Gobi, it sticks to the ribs. You can imagine the joy of being twenty, stuffing oneself with it, drinking barrels of hot wine, and reeling and belching happily into a snowy alleyway in old Peking. I would never have done anything when young if I'd known how much I was going to miss it when old. Or the other way around: should have stayed in Peking and raised a brilliant brood. Maybe wandered up to Outer Mongolia and opened a sheepskin shop: jackets, bootees, good stout trousers, the works.

Mongolian Hot-Pot (huo-kuoerth, "fire-pot," pr. hwaw-gwawr), sometimes called "chrysanthemum pot" by the provincial or insolent. The pot itself is an Oriental chafing dish, a chimney of brass above a small enclosed hearth, with a basin ringing the chimney. Fill basin with water and light your charcoal fire. While waiting for the boil, mutter ancient wisdom, e.g., never light the fire below an empty basin or the metal may crack when you add cold water. Slice into ⅛-inch strips, 1x2 inches to 2x3 inches, 1 pound lean beef and 1 pound lean lamb, to serve 8. (Pork never, as much of Mongolia and the Chinese northwest is or was Mohammedan; and chicken is too bland.) With chopsticks drop a strip or two into the boiling water. In 15 or 30 seconds it will be cooked. Drop in another, fish out the first and (a) dip it into your sauce and gobble it, or (b) slice a sesame bun halfway, stuff the sauced meat within, and eat the "sandwich."

The sauce: pour a dollop of each of these into your bowl, one at a time and with care, so they form colorful concentric circles: peanut oil (start with this), plum sauce, duck sauce, sweet and sour sauce, sesame oil, soy sauce, and a couple of dashes of white vinegar. At the first dip, your work of art will schmier, but you will shortly be too happy to care, and in time comatose. (Those who say "chrysanthemum pot" often add herbs.)

The sesame buns: take any hot-roll mix and roll it out onto a board generously sown with sesame seeds. Slice thin rounds about 3 inches in diameter and butter the inner 2-inch circle; slap the buttered sides together and join the edges firmly to make a coherent bun that will slice open gratefully. Bake as usual.

When the meat has disappeared and the guests look forlorn, drop half-cooked glass noodles and Chinese cabbage into the bubbling broth. By the time it re-bubbles (a minute or so) the vegetables will be soft; spoon this celestial soup into your bowl, adding it to the residual sauce, and enjoy it. Slurping is not merely permitted but complimentary. (Most of China takes soup at the end of the meal, so as not to insult the belly with premature and nonessential fillers—famine is a stern old teacher—and also pour rincer la bouche.)

Any dessert will do but it should be light and sweet. A slice of melon is both tasty and indigenous, and sherbet is also appropriate (up by Dead Mongol Pass, flavored snow). The best beverage is hot rice wine, the Japanese sake, or the Chinese huang-chiu ("yellow wine"). Next best is a toss-up between green tea (unfermented, like Dragon Well tea), oolong (semifermented, like jasmine tea), and lager beer. Avoid black teas (like the Iron Goddess of Mercy) and smoky teas (like Lapsang Souchong), as they tend to overpower the delicate commingling of flavors. The old Kirin beer is fine; so is the new Tsingtao.

Now serve moist hot towels. Allow 1 hour for borborygmus and eructation.

Golumbki

Gary Gildner

Golumbki are Polish and are also called Stuffed Cabbage and people who eat them usually eat them at the main meal but I have had them for breakfast too and been made happy all day.

You should find a large head of cabbage, preferably from the garden, and steam it until the leaves peel off easily. While it's steaming, brown ½ pound of ground beef and ½ pound of ground lamb in a big iron skillet and drain off the fat; cook some rice—wild is best—and sauté fresh garlic and chopped onion and a little chopped green pepper and carrot in butter. Be generous with the fresh pepper over the meat. If there are other seasonings you like and think will be interesting in this dish, add them.

Mix the meat, rice, and garlic/vegetables in the iron skillet; let these things get to know each other a little; add a fresh egg or two at the end.

Then peel off a leaf of cabbage and spoon a dollop of the mix onto it and wrap. Repeat (your wrap improving) until you run out of stuff. Place the wrapped cabbages in a pan, pour your favorite tomato sauce over the collection (be generous), cover the pan, and bake the golumbki for about an hour at 300° or so.

They are good all by themselves or with an ordinary red table wine and friends.

Hamburger

Louise Glück

    i can't wait to see what lenny
[Leonard Michaels] contrib-
utes. he does a wonderful boiled
hamburger. you start with a
rectangle of frozen meat, which
you take pains not to defrost.
you put it in a skillet. to hasten
its thawing, now suddenly
desirable, you cover it with
water. it turns gray. you mash
it up with a fork. you flee.

Medieval Beef

Jorie Graham

    Brown 2 pounds heavily floured and seasoned stew beef
in butter and bacon fat; put aside.
    Sauté mixed diced vegetables (1 cup carrots, 1 cup celery,
handful of chopped parsley, handful of shallots) in the
original pan.

Return beef cubes, add, when well heated again, 1 cup rum (dark, Bacardi), light on fire, toss a bit as it flames.

Add 2 tablespoons nutmeg (ground), 1 tablespoon ground pepper, and (optional) 2 tablespoons diced candied ginger or chutney.

Add another cup of rum, stir well (should be thickening considerably).

Add 2 cups light chicken broth.

Cook 2 hours (low flame).

Add 8 healthy cloves of garlic, thinly sliced.

Cook another hour and a half (or until done, depends on beef).

Before serving taste and correct for salt, nutmeg, pepper—and spice up if necessary with a few tablespoons of rum.

Serve with yams or rice.

(Can be made with more rum and less broth. And ground coriander can be added to nutmeg.)

Writer's Outdoor Meal

Doris Grumbach

Well, let me declare at once that I am not a cook. I can offer fervent, firsthand testimony to this fact from my many daughters, all of whom defended themselves and their palates against this patent truth by becoming excellent cooks themselves, and from my ex-husband who wisely chose a good cook for his second wife and seems very well pleased with his choice.

But because I must live I *do* cook, reluctantly, badly, forgetfully, and resentfully. Studying what I do when I cook, I discover that my main fault is a deep reluctance to cook *only*. I want to be doing something else while I am going through what I have always found to be boring, repetitive, and uninteresting motions like stirring, chopping, blending, and most of all *watching*. The result is that, invariably, I burn, or I scorch, or I cook too long, thus reducing everything to flaccid and flabby tastelessness, or to gray, well-done slabs.

So my success with the following menu is a result of having found something that I can do while doing something else I like to do, that is, sit in the sun and acquire a tan. My pleasure in this recipe lies in the fact that, if the dinner fails, something else, the tan, usually does not, and I regard that as success. (I would only add that I also like to write in the sun, for the same reason: if the prose is a total loss I come away glowing with health.)

Choose the sunniest spot on the patio. Turn the grill so that the cook is facing the sun. Retire to deck chair also facing sun and contemplate a new chapter while the electric starter heats up the charcoal. Do not forget to plug in the electric starter.

When the coals are hot arrange on the grill six well-packed hamburgers alternating with six equally well-packed hot dogs. The reason for the alternation is that it looks to the outside that you know what you are doing and that real forethought has gone into this dish. Return to chair and think out the first few sentences.

When the smell of burning meat assails your nostrils, leap up and turn the hamburgers and hot dogs. Sit down again, adjusting your chair slightly so you are directly in the sun's rays. Send a relative into the house to fetch the cardboard containers of Greek salad, potato salad, and cole slaw you have thoughtfully purchased at a good deli the morning of this feast. Warn the relative (maybe it is best to make it a *close* relative like a docile child) not to bring the purchased food out in the containers but to arrange it artistically in silver bowls.

Seated again in the sun, consider the final sentence of the chapter. Call the guests from their assorted refuges (from the food?) in the garden to the patio table. Accept all the preliminary remarks, such as: "It all looks so good!" and "I'm always as hungry as a bear in the outdoors!" and "How do you find the time to fix all this when you are writing all day?" with gracious silence and, choosing a chair for yourself in the sun, settle down with your guests to eat. Jump up only when you remember that you have not removed the meat from the grill. Serve burned with the wry observation that charcoal makes everything taste good. Accept the decline of compliments with equanimity, knowing that the new chapter is well on its way and your arms and face and legs look as if you have just returned from Barbados.

Mexican beer is very nice with this meal.

A couple of years ago I was asked to be guest of honor at a strange science fiction convention: limited to thirty people, it was held on a small island in the Florida Keys, where the University of Miami maintained a marine biology station. The program was skin diving by day and partying by night, and let the science fiction fall where it may. The organizers knew I enjoyed cooking and offered to buy the ingredients for any dish I would care to cook up for the crowd. I sent them out for twenty pounds of round steak, a bag of onions, a gallon of sour cream, and a bottle of Jack Daniels, for

Boozy Beef

Joe Haldeman

(Serves 4)
Butter
3 pounds round steak
4 medium onions, sliced
1 pint sour cream
Cayenne pepper and flour
Bourbon

Attempt to tenderize the round steak. I use the blunt edge of a cleaver, scoring the meat on both sides. A clean 2 x 4 works all right. Cut it up into rectangles about 1 by 2 inches (the meat, not the 2 x 4). Melt a few tablespoons of butter in a large frying pan. While it's melting, put a few tablespoons of flour and a teaspoon of cayenne together in a paper bag. Add a tablespoon of garlic salt; how could I forget that? Shake up the bag to mix. Then put the beef in and shake it up to coat the pieces with flour. Brown the meat quickly on both sides. Turn down the heat and add the onions. Stir it up and cover for a couple of minutes. When the onions have turned translucent, spoon in the sour cream. Mix it up thoroughly, then gurgle a couple of shots of bourbon over it. Mix again, cover, simmer for about a half hour. Take the rest of the bottle and sit in a corner while someone else fixes the rice and salad.

This recipe is very versatile. Without the bourbon, it's called "Beef." With dark rum, it's "Beef West Indies." With brandy, it's "Boeuf Something." With tequila, it's "Carne Borracha," a dandy emetic.

Dolma
for Five

Anthony Hecht

My wife is a superb cook, and has produced, besides deliriously good meals and a splendid ten-year-old son, three cookbooks: a collaborative effort called *Gifts in Good Taste*, which contains recipes for gift edibles, a volume all of her own called, *Cold Cuisine: Summer Food to Prepare in Advance and Serve at Leisure*, both published by Atheneum—

81

(the third book, *Cuisine For All Seasons,* has appeared from
Atheneum to a warm salutation by James Beard.) As a consequence, I have done little cooking in recent years. But, like
many men who are not duty-bound to prepare and serve three
meals a day to a family, I enjoy cooking, and can regard it,
when I do occasionally cook, as an agreeable therapy and
pleasant alternative to, say, grading papers or other discou-
raging work. I've always envied my friends who are sculptors
or graphic artists, and who can converse or listen to music
while engaged in their most serious and important work; but
since the work I do consists entirely of reading and writing, it
must be undertaken in solitude and silence. So cooking is the
nearest I can come to the sort of manual achievements of my
artist friends. Hors de cuisine as I find myself these days, I
must revert to a recipe from an Armenian poet and neighbor
of mine on the island of Ischia around 1950, a cheerful man
named Constantine Zarian, who figures as a prominent character in a volume of travel reminisceneces, *Prospero's Cell,* by
Lawrence Durrell.

750 grams (or a pound and a
    half) ground beef
½ hot red pepper, or a judicious
    amount of crushed, dried red
    pepper
2 onions, chopped
Parsley, finely chopped
Salt
Grape leaves or large boiled
    cabbage leaves (Grape leaves,
    bottled in brine, may be
    purchased at specialty food
    shops. They must be washed
    clean of their salt before
    using. Cabbage leaves,
    softened by boiling, are a
    suitable alternative.)
300 grams (or 10.6 ounces) rice
25 chestnuts, shelled
5 quinces (in despair use
    apples)
2 handfuls raisins

Add to the meat: salt, chopped onion, chopped red pepper, chopped parsley, and rice. Mix thoroughly and homogenously and mold into globes roughly the size of baseballs. Wrap these in the grape or cabbage leaves; place, covered with beef stock, in a pot and boil gently 45–60 minutes. Then add chestnuts, quinces, raisins, and cook till nuts and quinces are tender. Serve each dolma in a soup bowl, garnish it with the beef broth, nuts, raisins and quinces (which, incidentally, should have been sectioned, like apples) and a squeeze of fresh lemon juice.

P.S. My recipe is submitted as a poor substitute for a rich entree meant to honor the memory of T.S. Eliot: "Rats Feet Over Broken Glass." It's not for everyone.

My Grandmother's Beef Stew

Laura Jensen

In February of 1982 I was invited to Oberlin College where I read to introduce my book *Memory*. It snowed. A student gave me a tour of the historic campus and the art museum. After we separated I went to the hotel for lunch, wishing I had asked him to eat with me. I ordered beef soup. When it came, I recognized it immediately as my Mother's Beef Stew, and I wondered how two recipes could correspond so well. I could remember trudging through the snow at home pulling my sled rope in my wet mittens and thinking about the beef stew we would have for supper—chunks of carrot and beef and potato. My mother tells me it is really my Grandmother's Beef Stew, and I can remember her cooking beef in water on her wood stove at the house where my mother and uncles grew up. The recipe goes nicely with a loaf of homemade bread and butter.

Stew beef (about 1 pound)	Bay leaf
1 can beef bouillon or broth	2 carrots
1 small onion	2 small potatoes
1 teaspoon salt	Frozen peas or corn

Cut beef into small cubes or pieces, cover with water and bring to a boil. (Watch carefully, as it boils over very fast.) Skim off the foam, then add beef broth, salt, cut-up onion, and bay leaf. Simmer about 2—2½ hours, then add 2 carrots, cut up. Cook another half hour, then add 2 small potatoes, cut up. Cook for 15-20 minutes, or until potatoes are done. Then add some frozen peas or corn and cook for a few minutes.

Beef & Beer Stew

George Keithley

There's a recipe I like very much, and will supply the details. (I was afraid no one would ever ask!) Besides simplicity and convenience, it has the added virtue of combining two ingredients that I"m very fond of. Hence the name, "Beef & Beer Stew."

2 cans of a flavorful "light" beer, such as Michelob or Miller
3 pounds of chuck roast, cut into small strips and cubes
1 dozen broiling onions, cut into quarters

To cook: I'll use a crock pot, and put the onions in first. Place the meat on top of the onions. Pour the beer over both. Then cook at a hot setting for 2 hours to burn off the alcohol.

Then cook at a low setting for as long as you like, up to 7 or even 8 hours.

To serve: I like to serve this stew with herb rice and orange slices. The stew can be ladled onto the rice, or served by itself, with the herb rice and the orange slices on the side. And of course, if there's any of that beer left in the fridge. . . .

Beef Salad

William Matthews

This is an adaptation of an Elizabeth David recipe; hers is a variation on a standard French improvisation with boiled beef from the *pot-au-feu*. The American equivalent would be leftover pot roast, and if you've got enough of it you can start this recipe at the third step. Elizabeth David claims for this recipe "plenty of character without being outlandish."

The dish takes a little planning. Ask the butcher a week or so in advance for a veal knuckle; one can be got, but not usually on demand. And cook the meat a day ahead, or the night before, so it can spend the night in the refrigerator.

4 pounds stewing beef
A veal knuckle (about 3 pounds
    with the bone in would be
    perfect, but let's not pretend
    we can be fussy)
4 carrots
2 onions
A *bouquet garni,* or some
    chervil, thyme, and a bay leaf
12 shallots
A huge bunch of parsley
3 ounces capers
4 medium-size dill pickles
2 tablespoons Dijon-style
    mustard
1 cup olive oil
Tarragon vinegar
2 tomatoes

85

1. Put meat, carrots, onions and *bouquet garni* or loose herbs in a dutch oven or stockpot; cover with water and cook over low heat for 3 hours or so, until the meat is very tender.

2. Remove the meat, sprinkle it with olive oil, cover it with foil, and leave it in the refrigerator overnight. Save the stock for soup making later on.

3. Here's Elizabeth David on the next step: "Cut the meat when quite cold into thin slices, narrow and neat, a little smaller than a visiting card." There'll always be an England, even when it's mostly there in memory. Set the meat aside.

4. Chop shallots and parsley very fine. A food processor makes this step very fast; doing it by hand is lulling and meditative. The right texture is almost a pulp.

5. Stir in mustard, salt (very little) and pepper, chopped pickles, and capers. Add the olive oil gradually, stirring as you go, and then just a splash of tarragon vinegar. The sauce should be thick and, if you've used enough parsley, green.

6. Mix the sauce thoroughly with the meat. Let sit for a couple of hours before serving.

7. Chop tomatoes ("which are there mainly for appearance's sake") for garnish, arrange them, and serve the salad.

Rutsala's Main Dish

Vern Rutsala

This allows for many variations but what follows is a basic recipe, with suggestions for variations.

In an electric skillet add oil, then chopped green pepper, wait a bit and add chopped onion; when these look right add: 1 pound ground beef (or Italian sausage, crumbled. Polish sausage is good too). Brown meat. Meanwhile prepare pasta—fettucine is good though any pasta is fine. When meat is browned add a can of stewed tomatoes coarsely chopped; then add garbanzo beans with their liquid and drained kidney beans. Somewhere along the way add seasonings: oregano, thyme, chili powder—I like the idea of adding dashes of things. A bay leaf is always nice. Add ½ cup grated cheese: Cheddar, Parmesan, Romano—your choice. Sliced ripe olives add a nice touch. Drain pasta and add to dish. Ideally the dish should simmer awhile though at this point it's ready. (If it seems a bit shy on liquid add a small can of V-8 juice.) Heat thoroughly and serve.

Note the absence of smoked oysters: eat those on crackers while you're cooking.

With dinner, a green salad and the best wine you can find or beer.

My recipes are top secret. The C.I.A. and K.G.B. have tried for years to get them from me. I've been tortured too. Besides, the ingredients are too exotic for a modern household. They are only to be found in the guts of a certain pig in the boonies of my ancestral Serbia. I appreciate your asking, though. I'm sure there'll be plenty of roasted nightingales, sausages or angelic liver, etc.

Charles Simic

Jerry's Stew

Gerald Stern

Jerry's stew may be pretty standard stuff, but it's the stuff dreams are made of. You take 2 or 3 pounds of lean beef, making sure the pieces are real chunks of uneven sizes and not ridiculous sterile cubes, a large bunch of oversize carrots, a gigantic yam, 2 or 3 sweet potatoes, 2 or 3 white potatoes—preferably Idahos—onions, fresh garlic, fresh mushrooms, fresh string beans, wine, oil, salt, pepper, bay leaf, water. You cook the meat in oil and onions over a large flame until it is practically burnt, then add a little water and cook over a low fire, in a covered pot, for about an hour. Then you add the ingredients one at a time, first the carrots, not cut too small, then later the potatoes, likewise not cut too small, then the beans and finally the mushrooms. Add the wine from time to time. Add the bay leaf in the beginning, salt and pepper later. There should be resistance in the vegetables. They shouldn't be overcooked, but the meat should be soft. It should be eaten immediately, with French or Italian bread and butter and a nice Romaine salad. Good red wine. Domestica is fine.

Jerry's stew, in addition to being a filling and healthful dish, is also a specific. It prevents unhappiness, it brings people together in true intimacy, it makes peace, especially between warring factions among poets, it brings true tears to your eyes. Arthur Vogelsang insists it is an aphrodisiac. James Galvin eats it before long ski trips. It prevents war.

* * *

POULTRY

* * *

Chicken Backs and Necks

Marvin Bell

I like the title: *Chicken Backs and Necks.* Right away you know you're not in the presence of a gourmet cook. You can relax.

I chose this recipe because I had already given to another editor my All-Time recipe: *Heavy Fried Matzoh.* When you eat *Heavy Fried Matzoh* at 3:00 A.M., as you should, you feel something. It's not art, it's eats, and you can get the same feeling by swallowing a monkey wrench.

In other words, I didn't list the pleasures. You have to find them for yourself.

The same for *Chicken Backs and Necks.* (You can include

Wings, by the way. Just as long as you don't get into the really meaty parts of the bird.) The pleasures are personal, not to say neurotic. The pleasure in telling you is bred of a light defiance. After all, there are different kinds of meals, and not just according to what food is eaten or how it is prepared. Everyone knows this in secret.

Chicken Backs and Necks won't give you much pleasure unless you can eat with your fingers, preferably while reading a newspaper. You should have only a modest knowledge of good wines, and a weight problem. This is a wonderful meal for weight watchers. Under 200 calories, it lasts, it crunches, it gives your hands odd shapes to play with, and it contains crispy skin and healthful meat, not to mention the sweetness of the Pope's Nose—referred to in a more religious time as "The Part that Went over the Fence Last." In addition, buying the main ingredients—pieces left behind, probably meant to be soup, cheap food among the butcher's favorite cuts—builds character. You are what you purchase.

You might as well buy 3–4 pounds, or about 18 pieces. That should make 3 servings.

Besides 3–4 pounds of chicken backs and necks, you'll need a stick of margarine, at least 1 tablespoon of poultry seasoning, paprika, onion powder, garlic powder, and celery salt—each added to taste—a pinch of basil, and a pinch of marjoram.

Now. Arrange the pieces of chicken on the broiler pan, skin side down. It's possible that this is the arty part of the procedure. Think of it as abstract art, or solid geometry, or loading a truck. I used to load trucks.

Melt the margarine and stir in the spices. Brush half of that mixture over the chicken. Broil 45 minutes under a gas flame, or until brown. Turn the pieces of chicken over. Brush them with what remains of the mixture of margarine and spices. Broil an additional half hour, or until the pieces are brown and crispy. At least once during cooking, remove accumulated grease and drippings from the boiler pan.

This may be a bit gritty for your taste. On the other hand, you can't order it at La Toque Blanche or at Four Seasons or even at Good Eats. I recently discovered, to my dismay, that Momma Matzoh's in Seattle serves a passable, if light, version of Fried Matzoh. No doubt it can be had elsewhere. But if you want your Chicken Backs and Necks, you will have to eat at home.

Chicken Ignorante

Stephen Berg

Out of kindness, I rarely cook. This first recipe of mine is the result of the family—wife and daughters—shaming me into the euphoria of invention.

Ignorante didn't poison anyone. In fact, after dinner, the women offered to buy me French lessons and a tall white hat and begged me to grow a pencil mustache. They even said they'd let me have the weekends off. They wouldn't stop kissing me. They made me a little paper crown. This was the important beginning of my career as the dangerously influential master chef of a right-wing cooking school.

Take 4 boned half chicken breasts and remove the skin. Place in a Pyrex dish in a preheated 350° oven. After about 7 minutes liberally squeeze fresh lemon over the breasts, spoon on small dabs of Pommery (moutard de Meaux) mustard, sprinkle about ¼ cup raisins and chopped scallions over the dish, give a squirt of good soy sauce to each piece of chicken, throw in perhaps 2 medium-size baking potatoes cut into eighths, then douse the chicken with enough Noilly Prat vermouth to leave some gravy when it is done. Dust with a little finely ground peanuts. Crown with roughs of fresh parsley. Bake for about 35–40 minutes.

Julia's Foolproof Chicken

Ann Birstein

This recipe comes from my sister Julia and is foolproof. All of my recipes come from my sister and they're all foolproof, this one even more so. I called her for it after contemplating the *Alice B. Toklas Cookbook* and realizing that I didn't have a syringe for injecting legs of lamb with brandy, or any hashish for brownies.

2 pounds chicken cutlets (boned, skinned, and split chicken breasts)
3 cans frozen orange juice, defrosted
3 tablespoons dried minced onions
½ pound butter or margarine
½ cup flour
2 teaspoons curry powder

Dredge chicken cutlets in flour, brown in half of margarine or butter. Remove to baking dish. Add another ¼ pound of butter to the skillet, and 2 tablespoons of flour. Brown flour. Add the orange juice, stir, and let it all melt down for approximately 3 minutes, stirring all the scrapings into the sauce. Add the dried minced onion and the curry powder. Pour over chicken. Cover with aluminum foil. Bake in a low oven, approximately 325°, for 45 minutes to an hour. Serves 6.

Serve with Minute Rice, yes Minute Rice, also foolproof, and a salad. Half of the preparation for this dish can be done in advance, with the baking done the next day. It tastes even better this way since the sauce seeps into the chicken. It's also good cold.

Karie's Coq au Vin

Clark Blaise

Eliot advised us to steal and never borrow, so this is a stolen recipe from the best cook I know, Karie Friedman, of Urbana, Illinois. She masquerades as a researcher, editor, and housewife, but she excels in Chinese, French (*haute* and provincial), American (especially jugged pheasants and hare), and the red and white Italian cuisines. We first met the Friedmans in Montreal (her French and Chinese years), but I'm glad to say Illinois has not dimmed her inventiveness. Like George Washington Carver with the peanut, she can probably do a hundred different things with any scrap, any unpromising can, any unnameable vegetable or cut of meat.

Her coq au vin is a plain, good thing, and plain good things are just about the rarest things I know.

1 can undiluted Campbell's
    French onion soup
Equal amount (save the can) of
    dry red wine (chianti)
1 package (6) chicken thighs
1 tablespoon cumin
1 teaspoon ground cardamon

The soup is salt enough, so no additional salt is required. Make sure the wine/soup mixture covers the chicken. No need to skin the meat; simmer over low heat in a covered, heavy pot until the chicken is done.

This is one of the few meals I know that is good by candlelight or sixty watts, for families or working singles, and for the amorously inclined tired of bourguignonne, stroganoff, or pastas mulched by hand.

Busch's Chicken

Frederick Busch

To be placed in the oven about 2 hours before dinnertime and to be almost ignored while the cook writes.

1 fryer, cut into parts (legs and thighs separated)
4–6 potatoes
3 cloves garlic
6 carrots
5 stalks celery
6–8 small to medium onions

Rub a small amount of vegetable oil on the bottom of a roasting pan, or on the aluminum foil you've laid on the bottom of the pan. Peel carrots and slice into ¾-inch pieces. Slice celery into medium-size pieces. Cut peeled garlic cloves into thirds or quarters. Peel onions and leave whole if very small; halve or quarter if large. Slice potatoes into 1½-inch chunks. Arrange all vegetables in pan. Place roasting rack, lightly oiled, on top of vegetables and place chicken parts on rack. A few grindings of fresh pepper, salt if desired, and then a teaspoon of thyme can be sprinkled on top of chicken and vegetables. Cover loosely with aluminum foil in a tent; allow for circulation of air under foil. Roast in a 350° oven. Remove foil during the last 45 minutes. Serve when chicken is done to your liking. The vegetables will be soggy with the liquor of the chicken. You will get fat. People will think that you can cook. Serve with a coarse red wine and a green salad. Serves 4.

Mediterranean Chicken

William Dickey

This dish may never have been eaten on the Mediterranean, but all of its ingredients seem to belong there. The recipe is a flexible and forgiving one, in that exact proportions aren't too important as long as a balance that pleases you is maintained: it can use more or less garlic, more red pepper or none. It can be eaten hot or cold, with garlic bread or rice or fettucine or boiled new potatoes. It keeps well in the refrigerator, is probably better the second day than the first, and freezes. And if all the chicken in your neighborhood should have flown away, the vegetables can be served by themselves.

The Vegetables

5–6 cloves garlic, crushed
2 large yellow onions, coarsely chopped
1 cup parsley, coarsely chopped
1 green bell pepper, cut in ½-inch dice
1 red bell pepper, cut similarly
1 pound mushrooms, washed, stemmed, and quartered if large
1 large eggplant, cut in ½-inch cubes
6 small zucchini, cut similarly
Olive oil
1 tablespoon salt
1 teaspoon dried oregano
1 teaspoon dried thyme
1 teaspoon crushed red pepper
Juice of 1 lemon
2 large (1 pound 13 ounces) cans Italian plum tomatoes, very well drained and cut in quarters

Cover the bottom of a large saucepan or stockpot with olive oil and heat to medium. Add garlic, onions, parsley, bell pepper, mushrooms, eggplant, and zucchini and cook until eggplant has softened slightly. Add spices, lemon juice and quartered tomatoes. Reduce heat to simmer and cover.

The Chicken

18 chicken wings, tip joints removed with cleaver
Flour
Salt
White pepper
Olive oil

Dredge the chicken wings in seasoned flour and brown them in olive oil in a large sauté pan. Drain on paper towels.

The Assembly

Add the chicken wings to the vegetable mixture, stirring to mix everything up thoroughly, and continue to simmer slowly until the chicken meat easily leaves the bones.

Strong's Neck Duck for Four

Richard Elman

Get a fresh duck, wash, and dry, inside and out, discard or, rather, reserve giblets, puppick etc. Season with freshly ground salt (sea) and pepper. Rub a fresh cut lemon all over the interior cavity. Squeeze juice all over skin. Season with crushed fresh garlic and borage blossoms (dried). Preheat oven to 400°. Place duck on a rack in a roasting pan and cook for 20-30 minutes.

Take the neck, the puppick, the heart, but not the liver, throw in a pot of water with salt, parsley, bit of borage, and a pinch of dill, and reduce from 1 quart to 1 pint by boiling. Let stand.

Take duck from oven, reduce heat to 350°, pour off duck fat into a frying pan, add chopped onion (about 2 spoonfuls) and the liver, salt, and pepper and fry, and then mash and chop into a paste. Reserve.

Turn duck and put back in oven for another 30 minutes; pour off fat.

Prepare a cup of bulgar wheat and 2 teaspoons of wild rice in a pint of broth and a half pint of boiling water. Reduce to soggy dry. Add liver paste to concoction and mix thoroughly. Stuff inside the cavity of the duck and return to oven for another 30 minutes. Pour off fat (be careful to save drippings, gribenes, etc. at bottom of pan) and return to oven for another 30 minutes.

Pour off fat, place duck and rack in a fresh pan, and return to oven for 10 minutes at 400°. Take roasting pan and deglaze on top of stove with clarified butter and white wine, or hard cider. Should make approximately a pint of gravy. Let duck stand approximately 20 minutes after roasting.

Serve with mashed turnips, dandelion or watercress salad, and Hargraves Vineyard (Long Island) 1980 Merlot, or any fine French Medoc, or California Petit Sirrah.

A recommended first course would be Long Island oysters on the half shell, iced, with fresh coriander and lemon.

Hope this does you. Good luck.

Bharati's Saffron and Yogurt Chicken

Bharati Mukherjee

As one might expect of The Tiger's Daughter, I had not been inside a kitchen until I came to Iowa City as a Writer's Workshop student and married a fellow writer. My knowledge and love of Indian cooking have bloomed entirely in North America.

4 chicken breasts, halved
2 onions (medium)
6 cloves garlic
1½ cups yogurt
4 tablespoons vegetable oil
A 2-inch piece of ginger root
1 tablespoon coriander
1 teaspoon cumin
1 teaspoon turmeric
1 teaspoon *garam masala*
½ teaspoon cayenne pepper (optional)
Salt
¼ teaspoon saffron
¼ teaspoon melted butter

In a food processor blend onion, garlic, and 4 tablespoons of yogurt into a smooth paste. Add the vegetable oil, ½ cup yogurt and all other spices *except saffon* and blend well. Pour into large bowl; stir remaining yogurt into this mixture.

Skin chicken breasts (8 pieces). Wash and dry thoroughly. Prick chicken parts with a fork. Embalm chicken in this

99

marinade. Cover bowl and refrigerate for 24 hours. Turn chicken several times while marinating.

Marinated chicken should be at room temperature when you begin cooking. Preheat oven to 400°. Place chicken and marinade in baking dish.

Soak saffron strands in 4 tablespoons hot water. Drizzle saffron and saffron water over chicken in baking dish. Drizzle melted butter over chicken.

Bake for 45 minutes or until tender.

To serve, garnish with quartered lemons and green chilies. Serve with boiled or fried rice.

Serves 4–6 people.

Red Chicken with Herbs

Jane Smiley

There are no good restaurants in Iowa City, but plenty of gardens. This is a recipe for September, when the peppers in the garden are turning red and there are still lots of tomatoes, but the weather is cooling off, so something hot tastes good. The best way of making this is with all fresh ingredients, but dried herbs and canned tomatoes aren't to be sneered at if you want to make it in the winter.

1 frying chicken, cut up, or 3
    pounds of breasts and thighs
3 or 4 sweet red peppers
1½ pounds ripe tomatoes
Lots of fresh tarragon
Lots of fresh thyme
Salt and pepper to taste

100

Wash, wipe dry, and sauté the chicken pieces in a little butter until they are golden brown on all sides. Core, skin, and chop the tomatoes; core and slice the peppers into narrow strips. Add tomatoes and peppers to browned chicken pieces and cook, covered, for 20 minutes. Uncover. Add tarragon, thyme, and pepper, and cook uncovered for another 20 minutes, until sauce is cooked down to a rich red. Salt to taste, serve with a salad and French bread to wipe up the sauce, and finish the meal with a big bowl of September raspberries, with cream from Moss's dairy. NOTE: My favorite variety of tomatoes for this dish is "Gurney Girl," and a good variety of peppers is "Tokyo Bell," which get very sweet when they redden.

Holly's Quail

Charles Wright

8 quail, split and flattened
2 skillets

Shake quail in salted flour. In each pan brown 4 quail in 2 tablespoons of butter and the grease from 2 strips of bacon, over a not-too-hot flame. Deglaze 1 of the pans (after putting all quail in the other) with 1 cup of dry vermouth and pour over quail with salt, pepper, and dried basil. Cover skillet with foil and bake for ½ hour at 350°.

* * *

SEAFOOD

* * *

Maryland Blue Crabs

Richard Bausch

I've got a delectable regional
recipe, my own variation on the
usual red pepper-style steamed
Maryland blue crabs. We buy
them live, bring them home in
a peach basket, and fill a trash
barrel with ice and water—the
barrel is lined with a Glad bag,
of course—then overturn the
peach basket; the crabs that
run are the ones we catch and
cook. These are sturdy
creatures (I once forgot a
dozen-bag of them in mid-July,
and three days later discovered
it in my trunk: six of those
crabs were still alive, and very,
very angry; Karen wanted to try
and raise them, keep them
somehow. I ate them for lunch,
gladly), so if you're quick and
careful, you don't lose any. The
meat of a blue crab is so delicate
and sweet, yet it goes bad faster
than almost anything; so we
don't cook any that aren't
alive, even though they
have been on ice.

Anyway, we get the crabs from the lawn to the barrel—I can hit the barrel from fifteen feet—by sweeping them up and tossing them in one motion, so you don't get pinched. You should be at least sixteen before you attempt this. Once they are all in the ice water, which numbs them, you prepare the seasoning, and the water. You need a large steamer, and I usually use a big peanut butter jar to mix the seasoning. You fill the jar with equal parts *black* pepper and celery salt (works out to four or five of those little spice jars of celery salt, and two large cans of pepper), and about half as much rock salt and dry mustard, with a little sprinkle of thyme, say a palm full. You shake this up in the jar, and when you take the lid off you've got the spice. Then you put about two quarts of water into the bottom of the steamer, along with two cans of beer, a shotglass of bourbon, and a couple of ounces of vinegar.

Then you wait, say, thirty minutes before you bring the water to a boil; the crabs are secure in the ice water, and—here's a secret—the ice water is seeping into the shells. The longer you leave them in the barrel, the more you'll have in the cooked crab. (Those who don't like the moisture, can simply begin the process right away.) At any rate, we born-into-it crab eaters like that crab-soup-like liquid on the inside of the shell: you suck the head, folks, and drink the milk of paradise.

After you've let them soak for a while, you take the top part of the steamer and, with a partner holding the lid under it, set it down next to the barrel and begin to arrange the crabs in it, belly down, claws folded neatly. With each layer of crabs, you pour in seasoning. The born-into-it crab eater usually likes the seasoning to be at a depth of about half an inch (in fact, around here, if the crabs don't look like they have been packed in mud, which is what they they look like with all that seasoning on them—people are unhappy); the point is you sprinkle the crabs liberally, liberally, with the seasoning, and you pour dry mustard on them as well. You should have, in a large steamer, about six or seven layers of crabs, which, depending on the size of the crabs, can be anywhere from three to five dozen.

The size of a blue crab matters less than the weight. There's nothing sadder than to see a neophyte paying twenty-four dollars a dozen for outsized featherweights, when for eight dollars he could have three dozen meaty regulars or mediums. Jumbo means, really, expensive. And while it is incredibly pleasing to get jumbos that are also meaty, it happens less these days than you might imagine. In any case, try to get whoever is selling them to you to talk about the weight. Crabbers usually know when the crabs are light.

When the water in the bottom of the steamer is boiling—and you shouldn't begin to load the upper part, really, until it *is* boiling—you put the top part of the steamer into place, carefully pulling the lid from beneath it; then you pour the water and seasoning that has dripped through the perforated bottom of the steamer over the crabs, and set the lid in place.

Cooking time is usually about forty-five minutes. The ones on the top layer will get done before those on the bottom, so be sure the ones on top are very red before you turn the heat off. Take only, say, five or six from the pot each time you and your guests are ready for more, and the new ones will always be hot. I usually just pick them out of the pot with tongs and use the lid of the steamer as a sort of tray. You can eat crabs for about three or four hours like that, drinking beer, talking, building up a matterhorn of shells on the table before you. Some people like a little bowl of vinegar, into which they dip the meat. Me, I don't even let the beer get in the way much; if you know how to do it, you can strip and eat a crab in such a way that you have very little trouble putting away a dozen or more. All you need is a knife and a small wooden mallet. ... But you'd better eat them, the first time, with someone who knows how to open and eat one. You're all invited over to my place on Saturday.

Zarzuela de Pescados

Eugene K. Garber

In the fall and spring of 1974–75 my family and I lived in the Spanish village of Nerja, about fifty kilometers east of Málaga, on the coast. The home we lived in was owned by a daughter of the Spanish poet José Guillén. Or is it Jorge? Up the street lived Francesco and Isabel Lorca. But we did not get to know these literary notables. We did, however, renew an important old friendship. Marvin and Dorothy Bell and their two sons lived next door for several months. We had a wonderful time talking, walking, not talking—too short a time.

Of the many Spanish dishes we experimented with, our favorite remains *Zarzuela de Pescados,* roughly the Spanish equivalent of bouillabaisse or cioppino, but better than either in our opinion.

3 tablespoons olive oil
3 tablespoons butter
1 pound halibut or other very
    firm white fish, skinned
½ pound shrimp
4 small lobster tails, cut in
    thirds or a dozen crayfish
½ pound mussels in shells
1 pound clams in shells
¼ cup white wine
1 medium onion, chopped fine
2 cloves garlic, pressed into a
    purée
3 medium tomatoes, peeled and
    chopped
    —Salt to taste
2 tablespoons minced fresh
    parsley
1 tablespoon lemon juice
¼ cup brandy

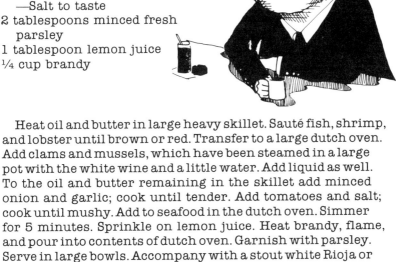

Heat oil and butter in large heavy skillet. Sauté fish, shrimp, and lobster until brown or red. Transfer to a large dutch oven. Add clams and mussels, which have been steamed in a large pot with the white wine and a little water. Add liquid as well. To the oil and butter remaining in the skillet add minced onion and garlic; cook until tender. Add tomatoes and salt; cook until mushy. Add to seafood in the dutch oven. Simmer for 5 minutes. Sprinkle on lemon juice. Heat brandy, flame, and pour into contents of dutch oven. Garnish with parsley. Serve in large bowls. Accompany with a stout white Rioja or a red like Marquis de Riscal or Federico Paternina. We prefer the red. Serves six.

Live-Broiled Sea-Spiders (for six)

Peter Klappert

*I'd like to eat a pair
of ragged claws . . .*

When I was at the Workshop I spent my summers at home in Rowayton, Connecticut. My parents were in Afghanistan, the house was empty, and at least a few times each summer friends came to visit for weekends or weeks at a time. It wasn't unusual for us to spend a day on Long Island Sound and, motoring up Five Mile River in the Rhodes 19, stop at Jean's Boat Livery for a couple of quarts of steamers and lobsters live from the big, galvanized holding tank. As I recall, lobsters went for $1.25 per pound.

Start with six lively and fractious lobsters, 1–1½ pounds each. Pick up lobster number one by gripping it at the back of the carapace just above the legs; make a loose fist with your own hand and rub the carapace, firmly and with a little friction, with the second joints of your fingers. It may take a minute or more, but gradually the lobster will stop squirming, let its legs and claws droop, and appear to go into a trance. Lay the lobster on its back on a cutting board and, with a heavy, sharp knife, split it in half lengthwise. *Be careful to cut to but not through the part of the shell against the board.* There may be some reflex twinges, some waving of legs: stay calm and bear down firmly. Now take the lobster in both hands and gently fold back the two halves; the intact part of the shell should flex like a stiff hinge.

Within the thorax you will see a pea green or beige organ that looks like a liver. It is a liver, called the tomaley. Remove the tomaley to a mixing bowl. If you're lucky, you may have a female with coral; remove the pinkish mass of eggs to the bowl. Next remove the long intestinal string and discard. Just below the head there will be a V-shaped, cartilaginous material; remove that and discard. Rinse the cavity and put the lobster on its back in a large broiler pan lined with foil. Begin hypnotizing lobster number two. Perhaps you would like to name the lobsters—Francis Thompson, Edgar Guest, Lois Wyse, Diane Wakowski, Kahlil Gibran. . .

You now have the lobsters split and arranged on the broiler pan. Melt 1–1½ pounds of butter: you'll need some for the lobster preparation, some for the table. Dice or pulverize the tomaley and coral in the mixing bowl. Add

2½ cups unseasoned bread crumbs
5 tablespoons finely chopped fresh parsley
2 tablespoons dried basil (or 4–6 tablespoons fresh)
2 cloves garlic, minced

and mix. Add

3 tablespoons lemon juice
1 cup melted butter
½ cup white wine

and mix. Add

1 cup cooked shrimp, broken

and mix.

If your broiler is small, you may want to start cooking the lobsters in the oven. In either case, begin heating the oven/broiler now by turning the thermostat to broil.

Stuff the lobsters, loosely at first to fill the cavities from head to tip of tail. Then press the additional stuffing in until it's gone. Baste the exposed lobster meat and the stuffing with melted butter. If you are using the oven, bake the lobsters 5–7 minutes before shifting them to the broiler, then broil another 5–7 minutes. To avoid scorching the shells, set the lobsters as far a possible from the broiler flames and cover lightly with foil until the last 3–4 minutes of cooking. (If you are unsure of when the lobsters are cooked—they should be a darkening bright red and the stuffing should be a little crusty—remove one and crack a claw: the meat should be opaque and firm, neither viscous nor dry.)

By rights, these lobsters ought to be preceded by a few bars of homemade French bread and a chorus of mussels or steamers cooked in shallots, fresh parsley, and white wine. They should arrive at the table along with corn on the cob just reaching a golden crescendo and a symphonic salad—leaf and chicory lettuce, quartered tomatoes, thinly sliced mushrooms and Bermuda onion, rings of green pepper, yellow squash in long wedges, watercress, and Italian parsley. Dress the salad in something breezy: a vinaigrette of lime juice, wine vinegar, and olive oil, seasoned lightly. And after the lobsters have been carried offstage, triumphant but lying about like heaps of old armor, let there be hot java and fresh fruit tarts.

John Leggett's Nostalgie de la Mer

John Leggett

When I lived by the sea, which was for a *very* long time, I gave all fish the widest possible berth. I did not angle for them, nor keep them in glass bowls, nor hang them on my walls, nor eat them. I prized steaks, chops, roasts, paillards, galantines, Chateaubriands, kebabs, and ate them at every reasonable opportunity.

But I am perverse of nature and when I moved to Iowa some fourteen years ago and a hospitable native asked if I was enjoying, "our good Iowa beef," I developed an overnight taste for seafood.

This is not a reasonable course, you will agree, because even the freshest sea fish when found in Iowa will have left his or her natural element four days previously and in Gloucester would be regarded as an old, smelly, and inedible fish.

Nevertheless I persist, preferring my former adversaries, sole, flounder, and haddock to the massive slabs of sirloin so highly regarded hereabouts.

What I do is this: stick to the above named clear, white, and relatively boneless varieties, taking them fresh when I can get them, frozen when I cannot.

Sizzle some oil, olive or safflower, in the bottom of a casserole or large skillet. Brown therein a clove of chopped garlic, a couple of onion slices or scallions also chopped. Reduce the heat to a simmer.

Add the fish, a half pound, say, thawed or frozen. Grind upon its bosom some fresh pepper, add a couple of bay leaves and a sprinkle of dill weed *or* basil.

Next, add half a cup of sliced mushrooms and, finally, slosh on half a cup of dry white wine. Cover and simmer over the lowest of flames for fifteen minutes. Serves two or three and they will almost smell the briny, Cape Ann breeze.

Gefilte Fish

Saul Maloff

This recipe is close enough to the version I was raised on as to make no difference.

When I went out to the University after World War II, my mother asked me where Iowa was, and as she wasn't much interested in maps, I tried to explain to her the *idea* of the Middle West—indeed of America as a continental nation. All she knew for certain was that it was located, if anywhere (there's a sense in which she was never wholly convinced it existed), somewhere west of her native Brest-Litovsk, and by that reckoning west of Delancey Street. And if Iowa existed, she wasn't wholly persuaded it was populated. "How is it possible to live there?" she asked anxiously on my visits "home." (Curiously, though, I had a family and "home" of my own in the recently demolished Templin Park "village" for veterans not far from the banks of the Iowa River, but I suppose the archaic brain situated "home" not there but at the

111

source.) Again and again I tried to persuade her that Iowa was not only populated but that it was teeming with splendid examples of humanity who not only lived there but lived very well amidst a bountiful nature, and that I felt for the state and its people a deep affection and almost filial loyalty. She wasn't listening. "Yes, yes," she would say, "but how is it possible to *live* there?" By live she meant, of course, *eat,* and by *eat* she meant food fit for menschen—fit for human consumption; and about that she had fixed ideas, none of them widely recognized in Iowa City, at least not the postwar Iowa City I knew best. Gefilte fish was one of her fixed ideas, and it was and remains one of mine. In a dark time, it helps make the planet marginally more habitable. My mother, whose first grandchild was *born* in Iowa City (though she never knew where it stood in relation to Lublin or Warsaw, to Vienna, or the Lower East Side of Manhattan), had no use for recipes—she trusted in the collective unconscious of our people and her own intuitive sense of how much was enough: a little here, a touch more there, and somehow it came out right. On an occasional rainy Friday afternoon before the Sabbath, I did the brute work for her: chopping and grinding the fish. After a certain number of rainy Friday afternoons, one learns. Here it is, my mother's prescription for surviving on the Iowa frontier.

4 pounds whitefish, carp, or
    pike (or mixed whitefish,
    carp, and pike) with skin,
    heads, and bones
3 medium onions, quartered
3 carrots, coarsely cut
1 stalk celery, with leaves,
    coarsely cut
4 teaspoons salt
2 eggs
¼ teaspoon white pepper
¼ cup matzoh meal

    Fillet fish. Reserve heads, bones, and skins. Dice fish; set aside for fish balls. (Diced fish should measure about 3 cups.)

Put fish heads, bones, and skins in a large saucepan. Add 2 of the onions, 2 of the carrots, the celery, 2 teaspoons salt and 2 quarts water. Bring to a boil, then turn down heat to simmer. Cover and simmer for a half hour.

Meanwhile, put diced fish, remaining onion, and remaining carrot through fine blade of meat grinder. Mix with remaining salt, eggs, ½ cup water, and pepper. Stir in matzoh meal, mix thoroughly. Chill for a half hour.

Moisten hands and shape mixture into small balls, using about 1 tablespoon for each. Lower balls carefully into fish stock. Simmer, covered, for an hour.

Remove fish balls from stock with slotted spoon. Strain stock over fish balls. Refrigerate until liquid is slightly set.

Salmon Joseph

Doug Unger

One of the finest restaurants I ever turned to for a job to sustain another month or two of writing is a place called The Fairhaven, in the small university and coastal town of Bellingham, Washington. From the moment I stepped into the kitchen of The Fairhaven—this time for a brief stretch washing dishes to keep my phone on and the lights from going out (my favorite quote from literature back then from Camus' notebooks, "Two years is not too long a time just to think about writing a novel")—I noticed a certain atmosphere of absurdist theater. Joe McConkey, owner and master chef of the place, creator of its multifariously excellent menu, presided over his kitchen help like a Pozzo to so many of us Luckys, a Hamm to all us Cloves. The dining room was often full, much of it for the seafood specialties (as Beckett put it once, "I see a multitude in transports of joy"). We kept a good banter up in the kitchen, the atmosphere as hot as a Sisyphian desert, the boutonniered waiters waltzing in off the floor like so many Brechtian gods stepping in off their clouds, broiling square pans stacking up at my elbows like Ionesco's chairs. But it was worth it. It was worth it if only to watch McConkey's famous dinners coming to life, and to take a few of his recipes with me when I made the transition from employee to patron. One of them is the best way I know to fix salmon, and a guaranteed solution to anyone's solipsistic crisis (the only item on The Fairhaven's menu Joseph McConkey has seen fit to name after himself):

1 large fillet fresh king or sockeye salmon
⅓ pound Nova Scotia smoked salmon (or Nova Scotia-
   style), finely chopped
⅓ pound butter
¼ cup lemon juice
½ cup chopped parsley
1 teaspoon cayenne pepper
1 tablespoon finely minced garlic

First, take the fillet of salmon, lay it skin down, and with a boning knife, make two long, parallel slits from about 2 inches below the head to about 4 inches from the tail (being careful *not* to cut through the skin). Combine the lemon juice and the parsley, then at room temperature blend in the butter, garlic, and cayenne. Turning back to the salmon fillet, fold in the finely chopped smoked salmon along its length. Lightly salt and pepper the fillet and lay the butter mixture generously into the crevices. Bake uncovered in a 375° oven for approximately 20–25 minutes, or until done. (The trick with salmon is *never* to overcook it—and I prefer it just slightly undercooked). Serves 6.

Sludge

Paul West

A reluctant gourmet, I can be forced into the presence of the exquisite so long as I get plenty of it. My friends tell me there thrives between food and me an almost psychopathic familiarity, which means that each winter I gain twenty pounds I lose over the summer. The trick, I've found, is to winter through on Sludge, which rather than a dish is a medium. Others have tried it and survived, although they tend to insist on the same ingredients not mixed together, whereas the essence of Sludge is Darwinian panmixis. You can make (and eat) it in your sleep.

Poach a pound of cod or haddock until it begins to break up, then add a dozen broccoli florets lightly boiled. Put in a pound of instant mashed potatoes made with skimmed milk and diet margarine. Turn and stir until the mixture is of even consistency and the pieces of fish are bite-size. Now mix in two poached eggs and add salt, pepper, tartar sauce to taste. The more broccoli you use, the lower the calories because there is less room for mashed potatoes. If calories don't matter, fry lumps of the mixture in a pan, both sides or all sides, and serve on French toast with small crisp sausages, even crisper bacon, flanked with heaps of black and lima beans, sautéed larks, pork steaks, and lashings of hashed browns.

This recipe works well even with fish fillets prefried in bread crumbs and frozen; the crumbs loosen and give the medium a crunchy tang while the lumps of fish slide free as if newborn. If you eat all of it yourself, you feel nourished for at least three hours, after which more of the same is recommended, possibly using scallops, salmon, or grouper (though for this last you may have to travel somewhat south and start all over again). Turbot is too slippery, sole too frail, whereas flounder being sturdier remains more or less intact until the final demolition. Some versions have succulent spring peas. Fresh whipped cream in the mashed potatoes opens up vistas of Sludge's more dangerous versions, favored, I'm told by at least one British prime minister, although her version uses hard-to-find Daddy's or HP sauce, a substitute for which is the sauce of Windsor, a bit sloppy for Sludge, or the mildest mustards of Barbados. For the Virginia version, take an entire Virginia ham, scoop out the middle until there remains only a half-inch casing, then cram with Sludge and stack the scooped-out ham on top in slices garnished with almost anything delicious that is bad for you. And eat it all yourself, allowing an entire afternoon; then an evening for recovery.

MISCELLANEOUS
MEAT
DISHES

Baked Camel (Stuffed)

T. C. Boyle

500 dates
200 plover eggs
20 two-pound carp
4 bustards, cleaned and plucked
2 sheep
1 large camel
Seasonings

Dig trench. Reduce inferno to hot coals, three feet in depth. Separately hard-cook eggs. Scale carp and stuff with shelled eggs and dates. Season bustards and stuff with stuffed carp. Stuff stuffed bustards into sheep and stuffed sheep into camel. Singe camel. Then wrap in leaves of doum palm and bury in pit. Bake two days. Serve with rice.

From Water Music by T. Coraghessan Boyle. Copyright © 1980, 1981 by T. Coraghessan Boyle. Reprinted by permission of Little, Brown & Co. in association with the Atlantic Monthly Press.

A few years ago at Sarah Lawrence, Grace Paley had an office opening off an old kitchen, and once a week wonderful things used to be cooked there for a seminar in American Studies. I would go to pick up Grace in the late afternoon, and our mouths would begin watering. Fortunately, one of the American Studies students was also a student of mine—a young Armenian woman. So when we smelled the very best aroma of all, we were able to get the secret of

MaJo Keleshian's Eggplant Moussaka

Jane Cooper

Serves 8

3 large or 4 small eggplants
½ stick butter
2 pounds lamb shoulder, ground
2 large onions
½ small can Hunts tomato sauce, plus ½ can tomato paste
Salt and pepper
Dried basil
4 or 5 eggs

1. Clean, peel, and slice eggplant lengthwise—½ inch thick. Salt each slice and let stand 1 hour to draw out the bitterness; wash and pat dry.

119

2. Melt some butter in a large frying pan. Chop onions and brown lightly; add meat and brown. Add basil to taste, tomato sauce and tomato paste mixed, salt and pepper.

3. Butter a baking tray generously. Arrange half the eggplant slices on the bottom of the tray, add meat filling, and cover with remaining eggplant slices. Cover the top of the tray with foil to keep in the moisture and bake 1½–2 hours in a 350° oven. (Bake until eggplant is cooked through. However, this is a very flexible dish, and if guests are late it can stay in the oven at a lower heat for up to an hour more.)

4. About 20 minutes before dinner is ready to be served, separate eggs, beat, and fold whites into yellows. Remove foil from eggplant and spread egg mixture over the top. Bake until golden. The eggs will rise slightly like a souffle. This will take about 10 minutes.

5. Serve with rice. My original handwritten recipe ends: "Serve and be prepared for thunderous applause!„

Champagne and Rattlesnake in The Whorehouse Room

Robert Day

In the main house on the ranch where I work there is a large room that has red wallpaper, a piano, ceiling fans, a chromed woodstove, old photographs of old cowboys, and a map of Kansas with a bullet hole put through Buck-Eye Township—where the ranch is—put there by an unhappy woman. We call the room the Whorehouse Room, and whenever we kill a rattlesnake we send to town for a bottle of Champagne so we can ring the bell in the yard and yell out: "There'll be Champagne and Rattlesnake in the Whorehouse."

First you kill the snake. Don't start shooting at him because you'll miss or blow a big hole in the back where the meat is. We've got a stout fence post to use. You pin his head until his tail turns up when it rattles, then cut off the head with a straight-edged razor. Clean off. Send someone to town for the Champagne.

Bury the snakehead in an ant pile so that in a few weeks one of the kids will have a clean skull to take to show-and-tell at school. Slit the snake with the straight-edge from stem to stern and clean him out. Feed the guts to the cat.

Don't cut off the rattles because you'll want those on the skin when you make a hatband. The women in the bars like to see a man with a lot of rattles on his hat and they'll come right up and ask for a story about how you killed the snake. Don't mention the fence post. The women will want to touch the hat, but not the rattles nor the skin. If your hatband skin doesn't have any rattles they won't have much to do with you.

Skin the snake head to tail by stretching him along a fence railing with a buddy holding the tail and you pulling the skin off while you keep the straight-edge handy to cut away the places where the meat sticks. It shouldn't take you ten minutes, but be careful when you get to the rattles because it gets difficult there. There's no trick to it, just go slow. When you get the skin free, scrape the inside with steel wool and tack it outside out to the shady side of the cabin wall so it dries with ease.

Go soak your snake in a sink of cold salt water and watch him twitch. They got electricity in their muscles and when they hit the water they get spasms and start flexing like they were alive. If there's a rookie around, or someone a little low on guts, you can get a cheap laugh by sending them to the sink to wash up the coffee mugs. In town they say we got the bullet hole in the map in the Whorehouse Room by sending the housekeeper to the sink with a skinned snake twitching in it. We did, but that's not when the shooting started.

There's some people who go and catch fish when they kill a snake so they can have a fish fry. If you do that, then cut up the snake in chunks and roll the chunks in the fish batter and fry the snake with the fish, it all coming out together fried. But Champagne doesn't go with fried food so we like to sauté our rattlesnake.

Wait about twenty minutes for the snake to stop swimming around in the sink and then take your straight-edge and fillet the back into two long strips. By this time the men should be back with the Champagne; put it in the freezer to get it cold.

Now get out the Number Eight Griswold and put in a little butter, not much garlic, some mushrooms sliced thin, and wait until the butter gets that brown foam to it, just this side of smoking. Lay in the snake strips and cut the heat back some. By the time the mushrooms are dark and there are bare spots on the Griswold where the butter's thinned out, the snake is done. Ring the bell and call out: "They'll be Champagne and Rattlesnake in the Whorehouse Room."

There's not much snake so you might want to bring out the peanuts in the shell and the Jack Daniels in order to ride through the rest of the afternoon in style.

Lamb Stew

Daniel Halpern

3 tablespoons butter
2 tablespoons olive oil
3 pounds boneless lamb
    shoulder, cut into 1½-inch
    cubes
1 tablespoon sugar
4 tablespoons flour
Salt and freshly ground pepper
2 medium onions, roughly
    chopped
2 cloves garlic, finely chopped
½ teaspoon saffron
2 carrots, cut in half lengthwise
    and then into ¼-inch slices
3 tomatoes, peeled, seeded, and
    chopped
1 medium potato, peeled and
    roughly chopped

1 small eggplant, peeled and cubed
1 cup dry red wine
¼ teaspoon cinnamon
½ teaspoon turmeric
1 teaspoon ground ginger
¼ teaspoon freshly grated nutmeg
½ teaspoon freshly ground black pepper
1 teaspoon paprika
1 teaspoon ground cumin
2 cups chicken stock*
½ cup chopped fresh parsley
Garnish: chopped fresh parsley or coriander

1. In a large skillet, melt 1 tablespoon of the butter in the oil and brown the pieces of lamb a few at a time, transferring them to a large casserole when they are done. Sprinkle the lamb in the casserole with the sugar and stir over high heat for 3 or 4 minutes until the sugar has caramelized. Add the flour, salt, and pepper to taste, and mix thoroughly. Place the casserole uncovered in a preheated 500° oven for 5 minutes. Remove the casserole from the oven and set aside. Reduce the oven to 300°.

2. Melt the remaining 2 tablespoons of butter in the skillet in which the meat was browned, add the onions, garlic, and saffron and sauté over moderate heat until the onions are soft, mixing well so the saffron is evenly distributed. Add the carrots, tomatoes, potatoes, and eggplant and cook until the vegetables have softened a bit. Add this mixture to the casserole.

3. Pour the wine into the skillet and over moderate heat scrape up the bits clinging to the bottom. Pour this into the casserole and add cinnamon, turmeric, ginger, nutmeg, pepper, paprika, and cumin. Mix and cook over moderate heat for a few minutes to distribute the spices and release their flavors.

4. Add the stock and mix thoroughly. The stew can be made up to this point and set aside until you're ready to prepare the meal.

5. Bring the casserole to a simmer, cover, and bake in the preheated oven for 50 minutes. Add the parsley and bake uncovered for 15 minutes to thicken the sauce.

6. Garnish with chopped fresh parsley, or fresh coriander.

*For added richness and flavor, add a few lamb bones when you prepare the chicken stock. This can also be done if your stock has already been made by letting the bones simmer in the stock for an hour or two, and then straining the liquid through a sieve lined with a double layer of cheesecloth, wrung out first in cold water.

Serves 6.

Scrambled Eggs and Bear Stew Brunch with Bloody Marys

Edward Hoagland

I enrich my scrambled eggs with tiny pats of butter scattered into them as they begin to gel, and then thicken them with Parmesan cheese sprinkled into the pan as well. My Bloody Marys I make with V-8 juice to which are added Worcestershire and Tabasco sauces and lemon juice. (The lemon juice is in commemoration of the Sicilian village where my first wife and I once lived. The little boys fell in love with her and broke off whole branches from the cruel padrone's lemon trees to season her breakfast tea—the padrone having woken us all up at 3:00 A.M. the night before by driving through this town that he owned with his horn blaring so that his gatekeeper would get the gate open before he got there).

The big thing with bear stew is, *don't shoot the bear;* or encourage anyone else to shoot the bear. Bears have enough troubles finding a place to live without anyone hunting them to make a bear stew. However, in hunting season, if I go to my neighborhood taxidermist in Glover, Vermont, invariably there is a bullyboy hunter from Hollywood, Florida who has just driven over from Lowell, in Vermont, or Colebrook, New Hampshire, with a newly dead bear cub in the back of his vehicle, and who is hollering how he wants it made into a lamp stand and that the mother bear just got away. He is pulling the cub's ears and stretching its lips and putting his fingers in the bullet holes to calculate the trajectory of damage and figuring out that the flowers it had been eating that are still caught between its teeth were jewelweed. The taxidermist and I both think that this bear should not utterly go to waste, so when he's skinning it, after he has persuaded the hunter to leave, he cuts off a meal for himself and a meal for me. This meat I dice into a stew pot with potatoes, onions, carrots, garlic, thyme, oregano, bay and rosemary leaves, adding fresh tomatoes and red wine and peas two or three hours later; and sample the concoction for supper; and reheat and really eat it the next day, smelling and feeling as strong as a pacifist can feel.

Roast Loin of Pork

William Kennedy

I generally leave the cooking to my wife and my culinary betters, but I do have a traditional recipe that you might want to use. It is a roast loin of pork, conventionally dressed, salted, etc., and covered with a quart of Irish whiskey. Cook for 3 hours, adding slowly another quart of Irish whiskey. By this time the pork is not edible, but the gravy is grand.

Barbeque Pork Ribs

Thomas Lux

The Sauce

One jar of barbeque sauce—any
  kind
John Turnbull's Spice
  mustard—about half a jar
Maître Jacques Dijon Chili
  Pepper mustard—about half
  a jar
Grey Poupon mustard—about
  half a jar
Molasses—2 teaspoons
Juice of 1 lemon
Soy sauce (Kikkoman)—not too
  much, darkens sauce
  considerably
Heinz Steak Sauce—about half
  a small bottle
Lots of freshly ground pepper
Worcestershire sauce—a few
  dashes
Italian seasoning—several dashes
Tabasco sauce—about a third of a small bottle
Optional: some pressed garlic
Optional: some fine fresh orange rind
(NOTE: do not use both optionals)

Mix this all together thoroughly. It will be fairly thick and
have a not entirely pleasant color. It will be very hot. Don't
worry about this—a good deal of the hot stuff will cook off.
Trust me.

The Fire, The Cooking

Use Match Light Briquets. It doesn't make a bit of difference
once the coals are ready to cook. Never mind what the purists

say. Also never mind hickory chips, or mesquite, or anything else like that. Good barbeque is in the sauce and the cooking. You will want a very low fire, bed of coals. This is crucial—pork ribs must be cooked slowly (*at least* three hours). My barbeque education is founded on this principle taught to me many years ago by the contemporary master (*il miglior fabbro*) of Pork Rib Barbeque, Michael Ryan. It is possible, of course, to cook them faster *but they are not as good.* So: smear (use a wooden spoon, not a brush) ribs (get good fat ones) with sauce and cook, turning every ten or fifteen minutes, until done.

Serve with green salad and Tater Tots.

Stuffed Derma

Saul Maloff

1 medium bunget, about 1 foot
   long
1 cup flour
3 tablespoons farina
½ cup raw suet, ground
½ teaspoon pepper
1 medium onion, grated
½ pound chopped meat
1 tablespoons paprika
1 teaspoon salt
1 carrot, grated
Additional fat, chopped onion,
   paprika

   Wash bunget, wrap thread around one end and knot well. Mix all ingredients (from flour through carrot) and stuff the bunget. Seal the end by tying with thread, knotting well. Bring three quarts of water to a boil. Plunge the kishke into the boiling water, then turn heat down to a simmer. (You may add a whole onion, skin and all, to the water.) Cook, uncovered, for 30 minutes, replenishing water if necessary. Line a roasting pan with additional fat and chopped onion; place the kishke on the bed of onions, sprinkle with paprika. Bake at 350° for 1½ hours.

I can't cook, go to cookbooks when I need recipes or fiction—and I'm almost as interested in the sound of the ingredients than their assembled taste. I did contribute a sort of recipe to a cookbook years ago. It was probably something like frying a hot dog.

Richard Stern

Squirrel Brains in Black Butter

James Tate

Six servings

48 squirrel brains
Salted water
1 cup beef bouillon
1 carrot, sliced
¼ cup sliced celery
1 onion, halved
1 bay leaf
¼ teaspoon thyme
½ cup butter
1 teaspoon cider vinegar
1 tablespoon capers

1. Soak the brains in water to cover with 2 teaspoons salt for 15 minutes. Remove the covering membrane and veins.

2. Drop the brains into boiling bouillon and add the carrot, celery, onion, bay leaf, and thyme. Reduce heat and simmer, covered, for 30 minutes.

3. Remove the brains, slice and place on a hot serving dish. Brown the butter, add the vinegar and capers, and pour over brains.

Another highly recommended way of preparing squirrel brains is Squirrel Brains Tempura, served with green onions, green beans, snow peas and sliced pickled radishes.

Both of these dishes regularly graced my childhood dining table. In fact, as a youngster barely five years old, I was forced onto the streets of downtown Kansas City by my great-grandmother, Delia Nail, and, armed with a single shot .22 rifle, I stalked my prey, the common ground squirrel, from sunup to sundown. Kansas City was still a young town, and the sight of a young bushy-headed tot picking squirrels off the roofs of the First National Bank and the Muehlbach Hotel didn't seem to cause much alarm among the bustling citizenry. But, still, even in such a free-spirited community, my shots were not always on the mark, and little wads of hot flying lead did occasionally find an unwanted home. I never actually hit a past, present, or future president of the United States, though I once nicked a school superintendent. The big, rosy-cheeked policeman who traced the bullet back to me was amused at what he found: at the busiest intersection in town stood a child-assassin in torn and faded bib-overalls, barefoot, and no taller than his rifle, with a gunnysack of dead squirrels that weighed as much as he did. I remember the sergeant's warm laughter when I told him of my mission: to bag ninety-six squirrels before nightfall or my great-grand-mother Delia Nail would bind my wrists and ankles with the coarsest hemp and leave me blindfolded in the cellar for the night to be nibbled at by rats. "Well, son," he said, messing my hair, "you're quite a little hunter. I just hope your great-grandmother doesn't decide to serve Squirrel Brains in Black Butter next Wednesday when Harry Truman comes to town."

Pig's Feet

Angus Wilson

Clean the feet and chop in two. Tie both halves with a slice of fresh pork fat between the halves. Wrap the feet in a linen cloth tied tightly at the ends, then cook them gently in a marinade of: half a bottle of white wine, salt, pepper, two or three cloves of garlic, a sprig of dried thyme, a bayleaf, one clove, a sliced carrot, a sliced onion, and sufficient water to cover the feet. Cook for about five to six hours, then allow the feet to cool a little. Unwrap them, and dip in beaten egg first, then bread crumbs. Grill turning often and serve with English mustard.

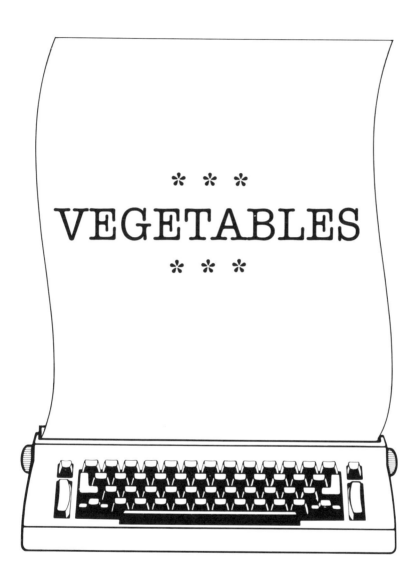

* * *

VEGETABLES

* * *

Brussels Sprouts with Garlands

Dianne Benedict

Here's what you do with Brussels sprouts which everybody hates: First you put a little butter (actually a *lot* of butter) in a skillet that loves food and doesn't try to scorch it. If you have a copper skillet, get ready for heaven. You add to the butter a little sesame oil (about 3 teaspoons). Then you add to this about 1 tablespoon of your best cooking oil. Into the oil (after you've got it heated up nicely) you begin to add and sauté the following ingredients in the following order:

Sliced shallots (½–1 cup)
Diced chives
Diced parsley
A little basil
A little cumin
A little mustard powder (gently, gently)
Sliced mushrooms (as many as make you happy)
Slivered almonds
Water chestnuts (sliced)
Sunflower seeds that have been roasted in tamari sauce
Sliced black olives
¼ cup yellow raisins

When these ingredients are sautéed just right, you add a little rum. Just a little.

Then come the Brussels sprouts. You will have steamed them (in a steamer where they are not submerged in water) until they are a little tender *but still firm.* (If you steam your sprouts to where they are soft, forget it. Throw the whole thing out and try baked potatoes instead—they're practically impossible to kill.) But if your sprouts are tender but firm, then drain them, and turn them into the skillet with the heavenly mix sautéeing in it. Stir this gently, gently, with the lid off (at no time in this recipe do you use a lid on the skillet) until everything just barely starts to brown. *Do not burn.* Have your meal timed so that you can put your sprouts right on the table as soon as they're done. Have a little sour cream on the side with paprika sprinkled on it (or you can sprinkle the paprika on the sprouts, which looks just as nice). This is a very good dish served with duck.

Rosemary Potatoes

Vance Bourjaily

This is a simple recipe which is going around the Southwest because so many people have rosemary growing in their yards. Out (t)here, that is, you can trim your hedge and cook the trimmings for dinner—but dried rosemary works just as well, and the dish is nifty.

Peel and cut up potatoes as for rather coarse french fries. Toss the pieces in olive oil so that each is well enough coated to keep the air away. Toss them again with rosemary, fresh or dried, so that each piece is sparsely freckled with clinging bits of herb. Spread the potatoes out in a single layer in an ovenproof pan. Let them stand for an hour, turning occasionally. Preheat oven to 350°. Turn the potatoes once again and slide the pan into the oven. Roast for about 20 minutes. Turn the potatoes and roast for about 20 more. When they are tender but not mushy, browning but not crusty, they are done. It's a little extravagant, because of the oil, but very good.

Vegetable Tempura

Michael Dennis Browne

Assemble some of your favorite vegetables and slice them long and thin. I tend to use carrots, zucchini, peppers, cauliflower, asparagus.

Combine in a bowl: 1 cup of *cold* water, 1 egg, and a pinch of salt and of baking soda. Whirl these ingredients together. Then add 1 cup of cake flour and mix up a lumpy batter. Do not be ashamed of the lumps—they come with the territory.

Add ⅓ cup more cake flour and stir it half-a-dozen times. Do not attempt to integrate it into the main body of the batter.

Take a larger bowl than the first and put some ice in it.

Place the batter bowl on top of the ice inside the larger bowl. This will keep the batter cool while you heat up some oil, preferably sesame, in a wok, to a depth of about 2 inches. Books say the oil should be heated to about 350–375° but I, having no frying thermometer, always guess when it is about right. If the oil smokes—too hot!

Using chopsticks or tongs, dip some pieces of vegetable first into the batter and then, when the excess has dripped from them back into the mother batter, into the wok.

Cook only 3 or 4 vegetable pieces at a time. When they are golden or so, remove them from the wok and put them on a rack, or on a paper towel, and then into a low oven to keep them warm.

Serve the vegetables with a dipping sauce. This can be made by heating up a small amount of clam juice together with half as much again of soy sauce and sherry. Grate some fresh ginger root or daikon and serve on the side—your guests can add however much they please to the sauce.

One macrobiotic cookbook I have proposes a sauce of ¼ teaspoon grated daikon or ⅛ of ginger together with 1 tablespoon of tamari and 1 of water. It also recommends ¾ cup whole wheat pastry flour together with ¼ cup of corn flour for the batter.

Marinated Eggplant

Nicholas Delbanco

Take three medium-size eggplants, peel and slice. (The slices should not be so thin as to crumble, not so thick as to be, later, opaque. An eight-inch eggplant could yield forty rounds.)

Bring cider vinegar to a boil—enough to cover—then pour it over the sliced eggplant and let it sit overnight. Next day remove and drain; then place the eggplant layer by layer in a glass bowl or earthenware crock. The marinade must be applied between each layer; do not skimp.

The marinade consists of olive oil *(pure)*, garlic chopped fine, black pepper, salt, cayenne or cracked red pepper, bay leaves, oregano. The quantities of each should be adjusted to taste, though there is no such thing as too much garlic; one crock can hold one bulb.

Make sure each round of eggplant has been covered, and the layers swim in oil. The dish is ready for serving in two weeks and will keep indefinitely—from the end of growing season to the time you plant.

Tomatoes in Cream

Robb Forman Dew

Pick 4 even-sized tomatoes from your garden.

Cut each one in half *not* intersecting the stem ends, but through the middle.

Melt 2 tablespoons butter in a large skillet until it bubbles.

Arrange tomatoes cut side up and sauté for 4 or 5 minutes.

Turn cut side down and sauté over low heat for 5 minutes.

Turn tomatoes face up once more and add ¾ cup heavy cream (not ultra pasteurized) and shake skillet lightly until cream and tomato juices meld and bubble. Carefully slip tomatoes and cream onto service plate and season lightly with salt. Serve on small, individual plates as a first course or with roast chicken.

Spanish Eagle Rice

Donald Hall

Warm half a cup of olive oil in the bottom of a kettle. Thinly slice two large cloves of garlic, maybe four small ones, and brown them in the olive oil. Then cut up three to four cups of onion, chopped in big quarter-inch pieces. When you have finished chopping the onions, turn up the olive oil and simmer the onions with the garlic, stirring them until they turn transparent.

Then add tomatoes, for instance a two-pound can of imported Italian tomatoes. (This is a good dish for winter. If you make it in August, for heaven's sake, use fresh tomatoes.) Then add a cup and a quarter of liquid. Usually I make this liquid out of pea juice (see below) and water.

Throw in anything else you want—mushrooms, fresh green pepper ... definitely add a tablespoon of chopped basil. Definitely put in a tablespoon of salt and a teaspoon of pepper. I cherish a dash of red pepper myself.

Then cover the pot and simmer it about half an hour. Brown rice takes longer.

When the rice is cooked, stir the whole thing up, and add a whole can of tiny peas, LeSeur for instance, or fresh ones at the right time of year. Then add a small can of chopped pimentoes and mix everything together.

This makes a fine vegetable dish, with a lot of mouth to it. You can hot it up a bit by frying a bit of sausage—around here the Portuguese sausage is probably the best we get; Spanish; good hard Italian sausage is fine.

Cauliflower Polonaise

David Hughes

This is an easy one for solitaries, very cheap and filling, and no trouble. Cut up a cauliflower into florets and parboil them until just firm. Hard-boil and roughly chop a couple of eggs. Make bread crumbs in the oven from a stale loaf and fry them crisp in sunflower oil. Arrange the florets in an ovenproof dish, sprinkle on the egg, cover with the bread crumbs and squeeze a lemon over the whole lot. You think one cauliflower of good size will keep you and a pair of guests quiet for lunch, but it's surprising how greedy you get—enough to eat the entire thing by yourself, especially if you grate some last-minute cheese on it. Drink strong beer or cheap white wine. Then try a siesta.

Avocado-Tomato Salad

Donald Justice

Peel and dice 1 medium-size avocado. Don't peel, but dice, 2 medium tomatoes. Add 2 tablespoons (or more) finely minced onion. Add salt and pepper, a few drops lemon juice, and 1 tablespoon mayonnaise. Serves 3–4. "Good for recuperation."

Salad Dressing à la Sylvie

Galway Kinnell

My house in Sheffield is two miles from the nearest plowed road. When I am there in winter I go in and out on skis, carrying supplies in a knapsack or sometimes on a sled which

I tie to me with a rope. One night in January 1973, in the midst of a howling storm, there was a knock at the door. Glowing with the exhilaration of her adventure through the storm, six feet tall, gorgeous, dressed in a glittering silver downhill racing outfit, Sylvie stepped into the room. She was a skier from Germany come to Vermont to race. My children thought she must be from outer space, heaven possibly. She had been sent by a friend of a friend. She stayed several days and made a great impression on us all. She left us this salad dressing. She used dried dillweed of necessity but said it is better to use fresh. A few years later Sylvie came to dinner with us in New York. Naturally I was very nervous about the salad. As soon as she had tasted it, she said, "I told you to use a *little* mustard and a *lot* of garlic!" In fact I was so nervous I had left out the garlic completely. Don't forget the garlic.

Vinegar
Olive oil
Mayonnaise
Mustard
Garlic, crushed
Dill and/or parsley chopped up
   fine
Salt

Pour the oil into the vinegar while stirring. Add the other ingredients and mix thoroughly. Thin as necessary with milk.

Potato Pancakes (Latkes)

Philip Levine

Here it is, in all its glory.
It's terrific. Eat well ...

Potatoes
Onions
Baking soda or powder
Flour
Egg
Salt

Copyright December 1972 by Frances Levine from
The WILPF Cook Book.

Use 1 large potato for each large person and 1 small onion for 3 potatoes. Peel and grate the potatoes on a hand grater. (Some people cut the potatoes in small pieces and pulverize them in a blender. I don't.) Drain the potato pulp until it's almost dry. If the pulp has discolored, forget it; it has nothing to do with the taste. Add 1 egg, 1 teaspoon of salt, 1 tablespoon of flour, and a pinch of baking soda or powder for every 2 cups of pulp, and mix well. Fry in hot oil in a heavy iron skillet over a medium-high fire. Turn when the edges are brown and crisp. For the greater glory, keep the latkes thin.

Serve with pot roast and accompany with sour cream and applesauce.

142

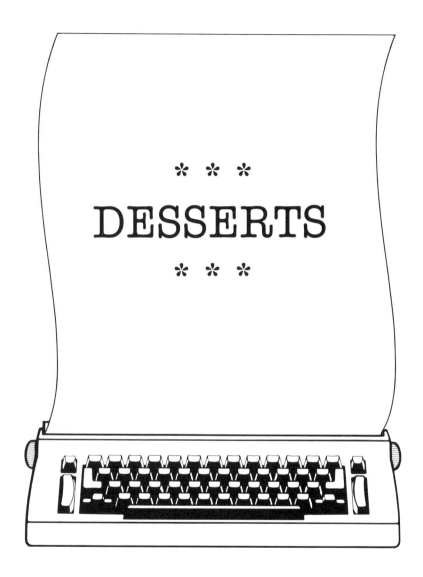

DESSERTS

The secret to good cooking resides in the cook's ability to say "the hell with the basic recipe" and improvise freely from it. If you haven't got this kind of moxie, you might as well hang up your apron. My model of a master chef is Leo, an itinerant chef whom I met in Rockport, Massachusetts, in the summer of 1965. I worked as his salad girl, and he taught me how to let the *feelings* I had for my guests flow into the food. That is the great secret.

Sweet Potato Pie

James Alan McPherson

2 medium-size yams
  (or sweet potatoes)
1 cup milk
  (or canned cream)
1 block of butter (real)
1 cup brown sugar
1 teaspoon vanilla extract
2 teaspoons lemon extract
2 eggs, well beaten
2 tablespoons cinnamon
  sugar

Boil yams until done (should be soft at centers). Blend with butter, eggs, sugar, extracts, etc. Blend thoroughly until batter is smooth (without lumps of potatoes, sugar). Let sit for ½ hour. Pour into an 8-inch pie pan and bake at 350° until done. (When done, centers of pie should be solid.)

My Mama taught me the basic recipe. My sister, Mary, has been reminding me of it for upwards of 20 years.

Christmas Pudding Maude-Helene

Janet Burroway

Christmas Pudding Maude-Helene is so called because it was concocted by combining the Christmas pudding recipes of my Arizonan grandmother and my Belgian grandmother-in-law, which seemed politic at the time but serendipitously produced a better batter than I've run into on either side of the Atlantic: lighter than the Belgian, richer than the Arizonan, spicier than either (my contribution). I usually make it in October, double the recipe below and divide it into one two-pound bowl and four or five one-pound bowls, so we can have the first one at Thanksgiving and the last around Easter. It'll keep.

1 cup ground suet
1 cup ground raisins
½ cup chopped figs
½ cup chopped dates
1½ cups ground or grated carrots
½ cup chopped nutmeats
¾ cup molasses
1 beaten egg
½ teaspoon soda
2 teaspoons cinnamon
1½ teaspoons ginger
½ teaspoon ground cloves
1 cup flour
½ cup dry bread crumbs
¼ cup rum
Juice of 1 lemon, grated zest

145

Dump it all together and mix. Divide into buttered glass or pottery ovenproof bowls, filling each about ⅔ full. Cover with aluminum foil, tie a string tightly around the rim and crush the aluminum foil back up over the string. Place each bowl in a pan with about 2 inches of water and steam for 2½ hours. When ready to serve, steam again for ½ hour, remove foil, and upend on a serving plate. Optional (but the best of the fun): pour ¼ to ½ cup heated brandy over the mound and set aflame.

Serve with a liberal dollop of hard sauce or brandy butter.

Mousse & Menthe

Janet Burroway

Mousse & Menthe is also an Americanized version of a *mousse au chocolat* I began making in Belgium, but I don't remember the source of the recipe. This one is quick to make but very quickly consumed. The quantity below will fill about ten champagne glasses.

8 ounces semisweet chocolate chips
4 tablespoons cool water
10 eggs
2 tablespoons brandy
6 Nice biscuits or, failing that, vanilla wafers, finely crushed
3–4 tablespoons crème de menthe

Separate the eggs; whip whites stiff. Melt the chocolate chips in a double boiler, remove from fire but leave over the hot water. Add the water 1 tablespoon at a time and whisk vigorously. The chocolate will seem to harden and get lumpy but don't panic. Just remove from heat, keep whisking, and add the yolks one at a time; it will turn smooth and creamy. Add the brandy, stir. Fold into the egg whites and stir until smooth.

Into each goblet put a scant teaspoon of the cookie crumbs, then a liberal teaspoon of the crème de menthe, which the crumbs will absorb. Spoon the mousse on top of this and refrigerate for at least 2 hours. Serve very cold, and if you can't resist it (I can't), with a tablespoon of fresh whipped cream.

Royal Marble Cheesecake

Rita Dove

In 1976, I visited New York for the first time—a wary and green midwesterner fully expecting to have my purse snatched. Instead, I was the recipient of generosity from a stranger. One evening, at the home of James Reiss, my former poetry teacher, I met a woman who, surprised that I had not yet sampled New York cheesecake, offered to send me a special recipe. Although I didn't really expect a follow-up from such a "party conversation," the recipe showed up in my mail ten days later. Thank you, Leslie B. Mechanic!

A six-ounce package semisweet chocolate chips
1 cup flour
1 cup plus 2 tablespoons sugar
½ teaspoon salt
¼ cup butter or margarine
3 8-ounce packages cream cheese
2 teaspoons vanilla
6 eggs
1 cup sour cream

1. Preheat oven to 400°. Melt chocolate in top of double boiler. Combine ¾ cup flour, 2 tablespoons sugar, and salt; cut in butter until particles are fine. Stir in 2 tablespoons melted chocolate. Press dough onto bottom of 9-inch springform pan. Bake at 400° for 10 minutes.
2. Soften cream cheese with 1 cup sugar. Blend in ¼ cup flour and the vanilla. Add eggs, one at a time, beating well after each addition. Blend in sour cream.

147

3. Combine remaining chocolate with 1¾ cups of cheese mixture. Pour half of plain mixture over crust. Top with spoonfuls of half the chocolate mixture. Cover with remaining plain mixture and then with spoonfuls of remaining chocolate mixture. Cut chocolate through batter with spatula to marble.

4. Place in a 400° oven; immediately reduce heat to 300°. Bake 1 hour; turn off oven and let cake stay in closed oven another hour. Remove from oven. Cool away from drafts 2–3 hours. Chill 8 hours.

Grandma Catherine's Date Roll-up Cookies

(slightly updated)

Susan Engberg

Dough

cream: ½ cup butter

add: ½ cup granulated sugar (or less)
     ½ cup brown sugar
     1 egg
     1 teaspoon vanilla

Mix together and add:

2 cups flour
½ teaspoon salt
½ teaspoon baking soda

Filling

Cook until soft and thick:

½ pound chopped dates
¼ cup sugar (optional)
¼ cup water
1 teaspoon grated orange rind (or more)
Juice of ½ orange

Make the filling first and set it aside to cool. Make the dough, form it into a ball, and chill it slightly. Roll the dough into two oblongs, ½ inch thick, and spread each with filling, not quite to the edges. Roll up the filled dough into logs, slice off ½ inch cookies, and bake them on greased pans in a 375° oven for about 10 minutes, until just lightly browned. (NOTE: The logs will slice more easily if they are chilled for an hour or so; unbaked, they can be held in the refrigerator overnight or frozen indefinitely.)

Grandma's grandfather, Christian King, came from Pennsylvania to Iowa in 1847. In June of that year, he walked from Cedar County to Iowa City, which was then the state capital, to purchase forty acres of land from the government at $1.25 an acre.

One of Grandma's presents to us each Christmas was a double recipe of these cookies, brought to our house year after year in the same old Campfire marshmallow tin. Grandma lived to be 93; maybe you will, too, if you eat these cookies.

Uncle George's Chocolates

Paul Engle

I was blessed with uncles. One drove trotting/pacing horses on race tracks. One farmed deep in the northwest Minnesota woods where deer browsed for hay with cattle in the barnyard. One raised purebred Jersey cattle. One went west when young and settled in Pocatello, Idaho, where he made ice cream and traded his chocolates with the Snake and Bannock Indians for beaded moccasins. Every Christmas he sent us a box of many sorts of candies, always including a "fancy" box whose cover bore in living color a lady who obviously could not eat candy with her clothes on—my mother's conscience troubled her at the idea of a small boy contemplating such a wonder, but being of a disposition too generous for this world she risked my moral corruption by letting me open the box. Inside were huge chocolates of a taste so ravishing, a schedule for eating one every third day had to be established. "Can't imagine what Uncle George puts in these chocolates to make them so good," my prohibitionist Aunt Minnie would say (no liquor was ever allowed in our house, but now and then I would find a whiskey bottle on a string lowered into the cold water in the farm milk house, or behind the bin where very high quality coal for the forge was kept in the blacksmith shop). Minnie's grace before meals would always end, "And spare us, O Lord, from the terrible Demon Rum."

In Pocatello one year I met Uncle George's oldest friend, who was with him when he died in the Porte Neuf River while fishing. Uncle George had a heart attack and fell in the icy snow water. His waders filled, so that he floated downstream standing erect though dead, his rod following. Finally we talked about George's ice cream and candy store, where his friend had worked, hand-rolling those irresistible chocolates (I've never found their like again). "There was something special," I said, "in those chocolates. Do you know what it was?"

"Sure, but George never revealed the recipe. Now I can tell you beecause I used to add it to the mixture—it was the best white rum."

I never told Aunt Minnie. The news would have rushed her prematurely into Uncle George's presence in the Great Beyond, where she would have made a terrible scene.

Those marvelous boxes don't come any more, but I still believe that the best approach to chocolates is to find them beneath a half-naked woman whose breasts are being walked on by pairs of beaded moccasins for the children made by the Snake Indians in the Idaho mountains along the Snake River.

Pears à la Carver

Tess Gallagher

4 ripe pears (2 of these may be hidden before serving, to
    guarantee seconds)
½ cup light corn syrup
½ cup light brown sugar (pack to measure)
1 tablespoon vanilla extract (a lid full, roughly)
½ cup heavy cream
Chopped walnuts

Oven: 375°.
Peel pears, then core them from the blunt end.
Leave stem intact.

In saucepan mix sugar,
vanilla, and syrup. Cook 2
minutes until mixture thins.

Lay pears in shallow,
buttered, baking dish—on their
sides.

Keep them from touching.
Pour syrup over them.
Cover with aluminum foil.
Bake 30 minutes, turning once.
Uncover. Cook 20–30 minutes more, basting every 10
minutes.

If you sense a large, smiling presence in the doorway, speak
to it reassuringly, tell it there will be enough, and more after

that. *Do not* leave the kitchen during basting period! *Do not* allow anyone resembling this description into the kitchen with you! *If* the Carveresque figure returns, ask "What's in Alaska?" and it will disappear for a short time, long enough to transfer pears to serving dishes.

Retain syrup and pour into saucepan again.
Cook until syrup is darker and thicker, reduced to ½ cup.
(NOTE: The Caramel sauce would normally serve eight. This is not normally.)
Stir in cream.
Heat 1 minute longer, stirring while you look over your shoulder for the return of Carver.
Stand pears on blunt ends in glass dishes.
Pour syrup over the pears.
Garnish with walnuts. Or candied lilacs (optional).

Now Carver will be standing behind you with a strange gleam in his eye. (Hopefully you've hidden two pears.) Move swiftly to the table with the remaining pair of pears. Tell Carver: that's all there is. He will want to eat yours first. Tell him that's fine. After that, watch him move on to his own pear.

He will be speaking of himself in the plural by now: "*We* would like a little more of that, please." He may try to add ice cream to the dish at this point, when you bring out one of the hidden pears. To discourage this, be sure to put the pear in a small dish. He will be making little pleasure noises by now. But do not be fooled into surrendering the last pear. He has not had enough.

Wait until you see him firmly established at the window facing the neighbor's bedroom where he loves to sit. Then take your pear out onto the front porch steps and eat it, slowly, in the dark while you watch your neighbor with his flashlight, moving across his lawn picking up slugs in a coffee can. It is best to eat the pear with your hands because Carver is able to detect the clinking of spoons several rooms away.

NOTE: Be sure to have on hand a box of Swiss chocolates in case Carver, provoked by the pears, goes onto a real sweettooth rampage. He will be riffling the cupboards calling: "More, more!"
You will get the idea.
You will have to do something.
Quick.

Cake with Carrots

Christian Gehman

2 pounds butter
2 pounds white sugar
22 fresh eggs
2 pounds carrots
1 capful vanilla
1 tablespoon grated lemon rind
⅓ cup honey
2 pounds plus ¼ cup white flour
½ teaspoon salt
1 teaspoon baking powder

Preheat oven to 300°. Let the butter soften at room temperature. Cream it in a large bowl with a wooden spoon and then beat in the sugar (like a man possessed) until the mixture is very fluffy. Use a mixer if you have one. Separate the egg yolks from the whites. Beat the egg yolks to a lemon yellow froth. Wash the carrots. Peel them and remove the ends. Grate about four carrots. Puree the others in a food processor or electric blender with the egg yolks. Put this puree and the grated carrots in the bowl with the sugar and butter. Add a capful of vanilla extract, a tablespoon of grated lemon rind and a third cup of honey. .Treat all this to a severe beating with your famous wooden spoon. Sift the flour with a half teaspoon of salt and a teaspoon of baking powder. Beat it into the rest of the batter a little at a time. Beat at least ten strokes after each addition is incorporated. Beat fifty or sixty strokes after the flour is all in. You will be all in yourself, so sit down and rest for a minute.

Butter five loaf pans or two savarin molds and one loaf pan. Whip the egg whites to stiff peaks with a wire whisk in a copper bowl. Mix half the egg whites into the cake batter, and then quickly fold in the other half. Pour the batter immediately into the buttered pans.

Bake the cakes in the oven until they test done, or about one hour.

This cake is unlike any other carrot cake and is, in fact, one of the world's best cakes. It keeps pretty well and is great for Christmas presents.

Zabaglione Francesca

Francine du Plessix Gray

I add the Italian version of my baptismal name to this Roman delicacy because it is the *only* thing I knew how to cook when I finally dared to get married. Zabaglione has a reputation of being very aphrodisiac but this attribute is perhaps apocryphal. What I do know is that it is a marvelous energy-booster on those afternoons when the writing pace has been fierce, and one has not had time to have lunch. My novel *World Without End* was finished at the American Academy in Rome with the aid of many 4:00 P.M. ingestions of zabaglione.

For 4 persons:
6 egg yolks
⅓ cup sugar
⅔ cup dry sherry

In the top of a double boiler beat with a rotary beater the egg yolks until of omelette consistency; gradually add the sugar until very thick and pale in color; then beat in the sherry. Place the pan over boiling water and continue to beat relentlessly until the mixture foams up and begins to thicken. Keep beating the edges of the mixture toward the center of the pan since they're the ones that are going to thicken fastest. Be careful not to overcook. Pour into sherbet glasses, sprinkle with a dash of freshly grated nutmeg, add a fresh berry in the center if you wish for decoration, and serve *immediately* while still hot.

Lawrence of Arabia Rock Cake

Mark Helprin

Lawrence of Arabia Rock Cake used to sustain me when I was living alone in the woods. I would walk for many hours, with snowshoes and a rifle, and I often carried these rock cakes in my pocket. They're pretty awful, but they have a lot of calories.

Flour to taste
Margarine to taste
Sugar to taste
Raisins to taste
3 eggs

Mix in bowl until compound is smooth and creamy. Lightly grease a baking pan or piece of aluminum foil. Pour contents into a single cake. Bake in oven. Cut into small pieces. Lawrence of Arabia invented this, so don't blame me, blame him.

I'm assuming that by inviting contributions from "writers who have been associated with the Iowa Writers' Workshop in past years," you include writers loosely bound to you by ties of love and thought. The closest formal association with the Writers' Workshop I have ever had, as far as I know, was once, years ago, when I had a sinus attack while driving coast to coast and I stopped to have my nose blown out at the university hospital.

Swinishly Creamy Chocolate Ice Cream

X.J. Kennedy

You'll need a hand-cranked ice cream freezer. Plutocrats using an electric ice cream freezer also can follow these directions for making a basic mix.

5 cups heavy cream (2½ pints)
2 cups whole milk
1⅓ cups granulated sugar
¾ of a level teaspoon of salt—no more
4 teaspoons vanille extract
1 teaspoon fresh lemon juice
3¼ ounces (squares) unsweetened baking chocolate
3 cups rock salt
At least 15 pounds of ice cubes or 12 pounds of crushed ice

About 2 hours ahead of time, concoct your basic mix. First, melt the chocolate in a double boiler. Then pour it into a large bowl and add 1 cup of the cream (reserving the other 4), all the milk, sugar, vanilla, salt, and lemon juice. Simmer gently for 10 minutes, constantly stirring, then beat with a rotary beater, electric mixer, or wire whisk—enough to blend everything well. Park this bowlful of slop in a refrigerator and do something else for at least 90 minutes while it chills. Then whip the remaining cream till it is almost but not quite stiff. Stir it into the chilled mixture and give it a final whoosh with your beater. If you have to crush ice cubes, do so now; your mixture can meditate in the fridge a while without harm to it.

Now ready your freezer, cannister in place. Dump in the mix and pack the freezer, alternating 3-inch layers of crushed ice and chintzy thin layers of rock salt. Too much salt, and your ice cream will freeze too fast and turn out with the consistency of a Babylonian clay tablet. Crank for about 20 minutes, or until your arm wants to fall off.

Some freezers come with directions urging you to pack the finished ice cream down solid. Don't. To squash this manna flatter and tighter will only heighten the risk of its turning Babylonian on you. Eat it as soon as it's done. If you must preserve it till dessert time, smother the cannister with extra ice and bundle up your freezer in an old blanket. Let it sit. Don't even remove its dasher. If, despite these precautions, your stuff turns claylike, don't despair. Dish it out and let it melt for 5 minutes before you serve it, and it will be as slippery and smooth as a poet's grant application. If you make ice cream on a hot day, have spare ice on hand. This recipe makes about a gallon: a dozen swinish dishfuls or 16 to 20 sybaritic cones.

This is the recipe for a chocolate cake I once made for a faculty supper party at Jack Leggett's house. Jack drove me around Iowa City to buy the ingredients. We couldn't find the Presto Cake Flour, which includes salt and baking powder, anywhere, so I tried to approximate amounts, using another product. The cake was delicious, but pretty flat (about ¾ inch high). When it was served, a very, very tiny girl burst from its center.

Chocolate Cake

Hilma Wolitzer

½ cup butter
1 cup sugar
4 eggs
1 cup Presto Self-Rising Cake Flour
1 can Hershey's chocolate syrup (16 ounces)
1 teaspoon vanilla

Preheat oven to 375⁰. Grease tube pan and flour with cocoa powder. Cream butter, add sugar. Add eggs, one at a time, beating at medium speed with electric hand mixer, or rapidly with whisk. Add Presto, stir in well, and then mix. Add syrup and vanilla and stir well. Bake 40 minutes. (Test with toothpick after 35 minutes.)

CONTRI

Thumbnail

160

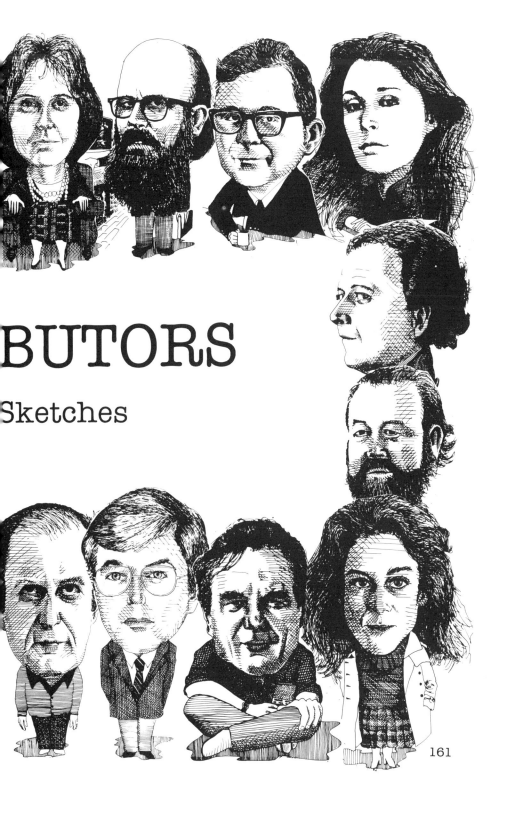

BUTORS

Sketches

Robert Anderson's work includes: Tea and Sympathy, I Never Sang For My Father, You Know I Can't Hear You When the Water's Running (plays); After and Getting Up and Going Home (novels); and The Nun's Story and The Sand Pebbles (screenplays).

Richard Bausch was a Teaching-Writing Fellow in the Writers' Workshop in 1974-75. His novels include Real Presence, and Take Me Back (nominated for PEN/Faulkner Award). His stories have appeared in Ploughshares and Atlantic. He was an NEA Fellow in 1983. His third novel, The Last Good Time, was published in October 1984.

Stephen Becker is author of ten novels (including a Far Eastern trilogy, The Chinese Bandit, The Last Mandarin, The Blue-Eyed Shan, works of biography and art history; ten translations (including The Last of the Just), stories, essays, screenplays, reviews, introductions, etc. He has lived in China, France, and northeastern United States. Anarchist. Animist.

Marvin Bell, author of seven books of poetry and one of essays, lives in Iowa City. Chicken Backs & Necks, he says, helped him to complete the Honolulu Marathon in 1979.

Joe David Bellamy (MFA, 1969) is presently professor of English at St. Lawrence University, where he founded Fiction International. His books include The New Fiction, Superfiction, and Olympic Gold Medalist.

Dianne Benedict is the author of Shiny Objects, which won the 1982 Iowa School of Letters Award for Short Fiction. Her forthcoming works include Gateway in the Fields of God, a novel, and On the Wings of the Morning, a collection of five long tales.

Stephen Berg is the author of Grief, With Akhmatova at the Black Gates, and other books of poetry. His new book of poems, On It, was published by the University of Illinois Press in early 1985. He is currently at work on a book of prose, Scarred Passions, and continues as co-editor of The American Poetry Review.

Ann Birstein is a novelist who invites a lot of people to dinner and then panics. She is the author of The Rabbi on 47th Street and American Children.

Clark Blaise is the author of two novels: Lusts and Lunar Attractions; three story collections: A North American Education, Tribal Justice, and Resident Alien; and a travel-memoir with his wife, Bharati Mukerjee, Days and Nights in Calcutta.

Vance Bourjaily's novels include The Violated, Confessions of a Spent Youth, The Man Who Knew Kennedy, Brill Among the Ruins, My Life as a Man, A Game Men Play, and the nonfiction book, Country Matters.

T. Coraghessan Boyle is the author of four books of fiction: Descent of Man, Water Music, Budding Prospects, and most recently Greasy Lake. He completed his MFA at Iowa in 1974 and his PhD in 1977.

Connie Brothers has been Program Associate at the Iowa Writers' Workshop for the past ten years. She graduated from Boston University and studied at the University of California at Berkeley, the University of Tübingen in Germany, and the University of Florence.

Michael Dennis Browne lives, teaches, writes, and cooks in Minnesota. His newest book is Smoke From the Fires (Carnegie-Mellon University Press, October 1984). It is not about cooking!

Janet Burroway's most recent books include the novels Raw Silk and Opening Nights; a volume of poetry, Material Goods; and the college text Writing Fiction. She is professor of English and director of the writing program at Florida State University.

Frederick Busch, once acting director of the Workshop, and its full-time fan, is the author of (most recently) Invisible Mending (a novel) and Too Late American Boyhood Blues (stories).

Mary Carter has published five novels and a lot of short stories, reviews, and articles; has recently finished another book and a novella; and is currently working up to a projected trilogy of thrillers (under a mysterious nom de plume, after the great literary tradition). After a decade of teaching around (Iowa, Boston University, College of William and Mary, etc.) she is now settled as director of Creative Writing at the University of Arizona in Tucson.

Laurie Colwin was born in New York City, where she now lives with her husband, Juris Jurjevics, and their child. She is the author of four novels and two collections of short stories. She has been cooking since she was eight years old.

Frank Conroy is the author of Stop-Time, an autobiographical novel. He is presently the director of the literature program for the National Endowment for the Arts.

Jane Cooper's Scaffolding: New & Selected Poems was published in May 1984 by Anvil Press Poetry, London. She was a member of the Workshop in 1953-54 and taught there in 1980-81.

Henri Coulette is the author of The Family Goldschmitt, The War of the Secret Agents, and Character & Crisis with Philip Levine. He received his MFA and PhD from the University of Iowa and has taught poetry at the Iowa Writers' Workshop.

Robert Dana is the author of In a Fugitive Season, The Power of the Visible, Some Versions of Silence, Journeys From the Skin, The Dark Flags of Waking, and My Glass Brother and Other Poems. He received his MA from the University of Iowa. He presently teaches at Cornell College.

Robert Day is the author of A Sampling of Poems, The Last Cattle Drive, Schyler, and Home Again, Home Again; LCD—in print with University of Kansas Press; and In My Stead with Cottonwood Press, Kansas University. He has a forthcoming novel, I Am in California and is writer-in-residence at Kansas University. He has received an NEA Fellowship; Yaddo; McDowell; Seaton Award for Short Fiction; brushes teeth with sidewinder rattles.

Nicholas Delbanco directs the Writing Program at the University of Michigan. He is the author of ten novels, a nonfiction study, Group Portrait: Conrad, Crane, Ford, James, and Wells, and a collection of short stories, About My Table.

164

Robb Forman Dew is the author of the novels <u>Dale Loves Sophie to Death</u> and <u>The Time of Her Life</u>. She recently taught at the University of Iowa Writers' Workshop.

William Dickey is trying to figure out how to interface two Osborne computers and a Cuisinart for a <u>nouvelle cuisine</u> that is high tech at the same time.

Rita Dove has published two books of poetry with Carnegie-Mellon University Press—<u>The Yellow House on the Corner</u> and <u>Museum</u>. A 1983 Guggenheim Fellow, she teaches at Arizona State University.

Norman Dubie was born and raised in northern New England. He is the author of twelve volumes of poetry—the most recent, <u>Selected and New Poems</u> published by Norton. He is a member of the English Department at Arizona State University.

Andre Dubus was born in Lake Charles, Louisiana, in 1936. He was a Marine Corps officer from 1958-64, resigning as captain. He attended the Iowa Writers' Workshop from January 1964-September 1966 and has taught at Bradford ever since. Books: <u>The Lieutenant</u> (a novel); short story collections: (1) <u>Separate Flights</u>, (2) <u>Adultery and Other Choices</u>, (3) <u>Finding a Girl in America</u>, (4) <u>The Times Are Never So Bad</u>. Godine published <u>Voices From the Moon</u>, novella, in 1984.

Stanley Elkin

Thumbnail Sketch

Novelist and poet Richard Elman is the author of <u>Menu Cypher</u> (novel), 1983; <u>Cocktails at Somoza's</u> (journalism), 1981; and <u>The Breadfruit Lotteries</u> (novel), 1980. He is a critic on "All Things Considered," National Public Radio and resides at Stony Brook, New York.

Susan Engberg, born and raised in Iowa, is the author of <u>Pastorale</u>(University of Illinois, 1982), <u>Stay By the River</u> (Viking, 1985), stories reprinted in <u>Prize Stories: The O. Henry Awards</u>. She won the 1983 Banta Award of the Wisconsin Library Association for <u>Pastorale</u> and the 1983 Fiction Award from the Society of Midland Authors.

Paul Engle was born of horse-training parents at Cedar Rapids, Iowa, October 12, 1908. He won the Yale Series of Younger Poets Prize and has written twelve volumes of poetry and eighteen other books of foolishness. Wrote section on Midwestern cooking in American Heritage book on regional American cooking. Prefers Chinese food. Greatest triumph of life—marrying Chinese novelist Hualing Nieh. If it doesn't have soy sauce and ginger, it isn't food.

Katheleen Fraser edits HOW(ever), a new publication exploring experimentalist directions in women's poetry. She founded The American Poetry Archive, currently teaches at San Francisco State, and has published eight poetry collections.

Tess Gallagher's third book of poems Willingly, has been published by Graywolf Press. She recently completed a film script with Raymond Carver and director, Michael Cimino. Her home is Port Angeles, Washington.

James Galvin is the author of Imaginary Timber and God's Mistress. He currently teaches at the University of Iowa Writers' Workshop.

Eugene K. Garber, a short story writer, directs the graduate program in English at SUNY Albany. There, as in Iowa, he remains in the debt of the students, who keep him running.

Christian Gehman won the Maxwell Perkins Prize in 1984 for his novel Beloved Gravely.

Gary Gildner's most recent books are Blue Like the Heavens: New & Selected Poems (Pittsburgh, 1984) and a collection of stories, The Crush (Ecco, 1983). He studied at Michigan State.

Louise Gluck was born and raised in New York and lives in Plainfield, Vermont, with her husband and son. She is the author of Firstborn, The House on Marshland, Descending Figure, and Triumph of Achilles, all poetry from Ecco Press.

Gail Godwin is the author of five novels, including The Odd Woman, Violet Clay, A Mother and Two Daughters, and The Finishing School. She has been both a student and a teacher in the Workshop.

Herbert Gold's latest novel Mister White Eyes, was published in October 1984 by Arbor House. His novel Salt is currently being filmed. He is well known for his modesty, compunction, and skill in racquet sports. His cooking causes people to shrink.

Barry Goldensohn is the author of Uncarving the Block and St. Venus Eve (both works of poetry).

Jorie Graham is the author of Hybrids of Plants and of Ghosts, Erosion, and The End of Beauty (forthcoming from Ecco in 1987). She currently teaches poetry at the Iowa Writers' Workshop.

Francine du Plessix Gray is the author of Divine Disobedience: Profiles in Catholic Radicalism (winner of the National Catholic Book Award), Hawaii: The Sugar-Coated Fortress, three novels: Lovers and Tyrants, World WIthout End, and October Blood.

Doris Grumbach concocts novels and criticism as well as recipes for avoiding genuine cuisine. She broadcasts reviews for National Public Radio and the MacNeill-Lehrer News Report (TV) to void both the typewriter and the stove.

Joe Haldeman's MFA thesis for the Workshop was the novel The Forever War, which won the Nebula and Hugo awards and is still going strong in its eleventh printing. He is currently working on a novel, a stage play, and a cookbook.

Donald Hall has published eight books of poetry, a habit which he supports by writing prose and making anthologies. Early in 1985, he published a collection of his articles about sports, Fathers Playing Catch with Sons (North Point Press) and The Oxford Book of Children's Verse in America.

Daniel Halpern is the author of four books of poetry: Traveling on Credit, Street Fire, Life Among Others, and Seasonal Rights, published by Viking/Penguin. He is a faculty member of the graduate Writing Division of Columbia University.

John Hawkes was born in 1925 and educated at Harvard. His ten books of fictions include Second Skin, The Blood Oranges, Virginie: Her Two Lives, and Adventures in the Alaskan Skin Trade. He teaches at Brown University where he is active in Brown's Graduate Writing Program.

Gwen Head is the author of Special Effects and The Ten Thousandth Night (Pitt Poetry Series). She is editor and publisher of Dragon Gate, Inc., and has just completed a third collection, Invisible Birth.

Anthony Hecht is the author of The Hard Hours (Pulitzer Prize in poetry, 1968), Millions of Strange Shadows, The Venetian Vespers, and A Love for Four Voices: Homage to Franz Joseph Haydn. He is the translator (with Helen Bacon) of Aeschylus' Seven Against Thebes and the co-editor of a volume of verse, Jiggery-Pokery.

Sketch of Mark Helprin, 30 words or less.

Don Hendrie Jr. is the author of the novels Boomkitchwatt, Blount's Anvil, and A Criminal Journey. He teaches writing at the University of Alabama.

Edward Hoagland Cooks and writes novels and essays in New York, Vermont, Africa, and Alaska. Past fifty now, he finds he has begun turning vegetarian.

Jane Howard is the author of Please Touch: A Guided Tour of the Human Potential Movement, A Different Woman, and Margaret Mead: A Life.

David J. Hughes is the author of a Feeling in the Air, Sealed with a Loving Kiss, The Horsehair Sofa, The Major, The Man Who Invented Tomorrow, and Memories of Dying (fiction). He has also published a book on J. B. Priestly, a travel book, The

Road to Stockholm, and The Seven Ages of England, a social history published in Stockholm.

John Irving was born in Exeter, New Hampshire, on March 2, 1942. He is the author of Setting Free the Bears, The Water-Method Man, The 158-Pound Marriage, The World According to Garp, The Hotel New Hampshire, and The Cider House Rules.

Laura Jensen received the MFA from the Iowa Writers' Workshop in 1974, and has since published Bad Boats (Ecco), Memory (Dragon Gate), and Shelter (Dragon Gate). Peace.

Donald Justice was born in Miami, Florida. He has taught in the Iowa Writers' Workshop for years and now teaches at the University of Florida. He won the Pulitzer Prize in 1980 for Selected Poems.

Edmund Keeley spends half the year teaching writing at Princeton and the other half in Greece or elsewhere writing fiction and translating poetry. His latest novel, A Wilderness Called Peace, was published by Simon & Shuster in early 1985.

George Keithley is the author of two prize-winning books of poetry, The Donner Party and Song in a Strange Land, and a verse play, The Best Blood of the Country.

William Kennedy is tha author of Ink Truck; the trilogy Legs, Billy Phelan's Greatest Game, and Ironweed for which he won the 1984 Pulitzer Prize; and O Albany: An Urban Tapestry.

X. J. Kennedy has published nine collections of verse, beginning with Nude Descending a Staircase (1961) and including four books for children. He has also written a novel for children, The Owlstone Crown (1983).

Tracy Kidder is the author of The Soul of a New Machine, which won both the Pulitzer Prize and the American Book Award for 1982. His most recent book is House.

Galway Kinnell teaches in the Creative Writing Program at New York University. He is the author of Selected Poems which won the 1982 Pulitzr Prize and the American Book Award for 1982. His other books include The Book of Nightmares and The Avenue Bearing the Initial of Christ into the New World, and his novel, Black Light.

Bill Kinsella, a 1978 graduate of the Workshop, has published nine books in the past eight years. His novel Shoeless Joe won the Houghton Mifflin Literary Fellowship in 1982.

Peter Klappert's collections of poems include Lugging Vegetables to Nantucket (Yale Series), Circular Stairs, Distress in the Mirrors, '52 Pick-Up: Scenes from THE CONSPIRACY, A Documentary, and The Idiot Princess of the Last Dynasty.

Maxine Kumin grows and cooks squash on an old farm in central New Hampshire where she also raises horses and lambs. Her most recent books are Our Ground Time Here Will be Brief (poems), Why Can't We Live Together Like Civilized Human Beings? (short stories), and The Microscope.

John Leggett has been director of the Iowa Writers' Workshop since 1970 and describes it as the best of all possible jobs. He is the author of the biography Ross & Tom and five novels, the latest, Making Believe, to be published in the spring of 1986.

Philip Levine is the author of On the Edge, Not This Pig They Feed They Lion, Seven Years From Somewhere, and Selected Poems.

Thomas Lux was born in 1946. He has published three full-length collections of poems as well as several chapbooks. He teaches at Sarah Lawrence College and rarely cooks anything but barbeque.

Robie Macauley's first job in publishing was on Gourmet magazine long ago. He is a novelist, critic, and the executive editor at Houghton Mifflin Company, Boston.

James Alan McPherson's books include Hue and Cry, Railroad, and Elbow Room. He won the Pulitzer Prize for fiction in 1978 and currently teaches at the University of Iowa Writers' Workshop.

Saul Maloff, a novelist and critic, has taught and lectured at many universities and colleges here and abroad. A contributor to numerous periodicals, he was books editor of Newsweek from 1964-69. He received his PhD from Iowa in 1952.

William Matthews is the author of six books of poems, father of two sons, a New York City resident, and an enthusiastic amateur cook.

Nicholas Meyer, born in New York City, adopted Iowa City (and vice versa). He is still trying to get something right.

Leonard Michaels is the author of three books: Going Places (stories), 1969, I Would Have Saved Them if I Could (stories), 1975, and The Men's Club (novel), 1981. He was born in New York and now lives in California where he teaches at Berkeley. He has two sons in their late teens and a daughter, six and a half years old, who is a promising singer.

Bharati Mukherjee is the author of two novels, Wife and The Tiger's Daughter, numerous stories and articles, an autobiography, with her husband, Clark Blaise, Days and Nights in Calcutta, and a books of stories, Darknesses.

William Murray is the author of the novels Michael Joe, A Long Way From Home, and Testimonial. He has written many short stoires and poems and produced a video film entitled Portrait of a Schizophrenic.

Carol Muske taught at the Iowa Writers' Workshop in the spring of 1982. Her third book of poems is called Wyndmere and she is currently at work on a novel. She recently moved from New York City to Los Angeles where she lives with her husband, actor David Dukes, her stepson Shawn, and her baby daughter, Annie Cameron, and is learning to cook.

Peter Nelson is a freelance writer/illustrator living in Providence, Rhode Island. He has published fiction in Playboy, Esquire, Seventeen, the Iowa Review, and other magazines. He wastes far too much money eating in restaurants, but when he cooks, he makes too much and has to eat it all himself. He once ate chili five nights in a row and gave the rest to his dog. The dog got sick.

Howard Nemerov is a hot dogs and beans (add raisins) gourmet. His recipe for Eggs Maledict is sometimes cited as a satire on American taste, junk food, etc., but in plain truth it is the kind of thing he eats, poor person.

Tim O'Brien won the 1979 National Book Award in fiction for Going After Caciato. His most recent novel, The Nuclear Age, was published in 1985.

Steve Orlen only cooks exotica with unpronounceable names, and only once in a while. His wife, Gail, has in her the charity and endurance and imagination to comb the cookbooks for their daily fare. He teaches at the University of Arizona, and his last book of poems was A Place at the Table, (Holt, Rinehart and Winston, 1982).

Grace Paley is the author of three short story collections, The Little Disturbances of Man, Enormous changes at the Last Minute, and Later the Same Day. She has taught at Columbia and Syracuse, and she currently teaches at Sarah Lawrence College.

Stanley Plumly's last two books of poetry are Out-of-the-Body Travel and Summer Celestial. He is currently working on a book about the last year and a half of the life of Keats.

Reynolds Price writes novels, short stories, poems, plays, and essays. His first novel was A Long and Happy Life, his most recent was A Palpable God. His first volume of poems, Vital Provisions, was published in 1982. He lives in Orange County, North Carolina, and is James B. Duke Professor of English at Duke University.

Vern Rutsala's collections of poetry include Paragraphs, The Journey Begins, and Walking Home from the Ice-House.

When Michael Ryan is not laboring over a hot stove or reading the newspaper, he writes poems and essays about poetry. His books are: Threats Instead of Trees (Yale, 1974) and In Winter (Holt, Rinehart and Winston, 1981). His essays have appeared in: American Poetry Review, Antaeus, Crazy Horse, New England Review, Poetry, and various anthologies.

Sherod Santos's first book, <u>Accidental Weather</u>, was published by Doubleday in 1982 as part of the National Poetry Series. His awards include the Delmore Schwartz Memorial Award, an Ingram Merrill Fellowship, and the Oscar Blumenthal Prize from <u>Poetry</u> magazine. Next year Sherod, his wife, and son will be living in Paris on a Guggenheim Fellowship.

Charles Simic is the author of ten collections of poetry, the last of which include <u>Austerities</u> and <u>Selected Poems 1963-83</u> both from Braziller. He expects raw onions and garlic to make him immortal.

Jane Smiley got her MFA from the Workshop in 1976 and taught there in the spring of 1981. She is the author of three novels, BARN BLIND, AT PARADISE GATE, and DUPLICATE KEYS. Unable, finally, to leave Iowa, she now teaches at Iowa State University in Ames, and is working on a novel about medieval Greenland.

W. D. Snodgrass teaches at the University of Delaware. He has just returned from six months in San Miguel, Mexico, where he was working on a cycle of poems about the death of Cock Robin.

William Stafford has been writing ever since his Iowa Writing Program days in the early fifties. Two of his poetry collections are current from Harper & Row.

Maura Stanton has published <u>Snow on Snow</u> (Yale, 1975), <u>Molly Companion</u> (Bobbs-Merrill, 1977), and <u>Cries of Swimmers</u> (Utah, 1984). She has lived in Virginia, California, and Arizona and now teaches in the MFA program at Indiana University.

Gerald Stern teaches poetry at the Iowa Writers' Workshop. He is the author of <u>Rejoicings</u>, <u>Lucky Life</u>, <u>The Red Coal</u>, and <u>Paradise Poems</u>. He is a Pennsylvanian.

Richard Stern does a bit better with novels than souffles. His tenth novel, <u>Men of Our Words</u> will be published in Spring 1986 (Arbor House).

Robert Stone is the author of <u>A Hall of Mirrors</u>, which won the Faulkner Award in 1967, <u>Dog Soldiers</u>, which won the National Book Award in 1975, <u>A Flag for Sunrise</u>, and <u>Children of Light</u>.

Mark Strand is the author of several collections of poetry including The Story of Our Lives (Academy of American Poets Edgar Allen Poe Award, 1974), The Late Hour, and Selected Poems. He has edited two anthologies of American poetry, and is the recipient of numerous grants and awards. He received his MA from the University of Iowa.

Mary Swander has a book of poems published by the University of Georgia Press, Succession, which won the Carl Sandburg Literary Award, another book of poems, Driving the Body Back, forthcoming from Knopf in 1986. She has a private practice in therapeutic massage in Iowa City.

Thom Swiss was awarded an NEA Fellowship in poetry for 1984. He is currently director of the writing workshop at Drake University.

James Tate was born in Kansas City, Missouri, in 1943 and grew up there. His first book, The Lost Pilot, won the Yale Series of Younger Poets Award in 1966. His volumes of poetry since then include The Oblivion Ha-Ha, Hints to Pilgrims, Absences, Viper Jazz, Riven Doggeries, and Constant Defender.

Anne Tyler is the author of nine novels, the most recent of which is The Accidental Tourist.

Leslie Ullman is the author of Natural Histories, one of the Yale Younger Poets Series books.

Douglas Unger is the author of the novel Leaving the Land. He divides his time between the writing program at Syracuse University and the Burk family farm in northwest Washington, where he is at work on a new novel.

Constance Urdang is the author of four collections of poems, most recently Only the World, one novel, and is now coordinator of the Writers' Program at Washington University in St. Louis.

Mona Van Duyn is the author of To See, To Take; Merciful Disguises; and Letters From a Father and Other Poems. She received her MA from the University of Iowa in 1943.

Arturo Vivante's latest collection of stories is Run to the Waterfall. Another recent book is Writing Fiction. He teaches at Bennington.

Dan Wakefield began writing Starting Over, his best-selling novel that became a hit movie, while living in a funky farmhouse in West Branch and teaching at Iowa. Except for Beacon Hill, Iowa City is his favorite place.

Paul West's books include Stauffenberg, Alley Jaggers, Gala, Words for a Deaf Daughter, and Out of My Depths, a memoir. His awards include the Aga Khan Fiction Prize and the Hazlett Award for Excellence. He is currently writer-in-resident at the University of Arizona.

Joy Williams is the author of Taking Care (stories) and State of Grace (novel).

Miller Williams's recent poems are collected in The Boys on Their Bony Mules. Translator of Nicanor Parra and Giuseppe Belli, he was awarded the Prix de Rome for Literature in 1976. He is director of The University of Arkansas Press.

Angus Wilson, the British novelist, loves traveling and teaching in America. His novel, The Old Men at the Zoo, has just been a great success in the UK as a five-part television serial.

AUTHOR	TITLE	RECIPE
Susan Engberg, p. 148	Grandma Catherine's Date Roll-Up Cookies (slightly updated)	cookies
Paul Engle, p. 150	Uncle George's Chocolates	chocolates
Kathleen Fraser, p. 9	Sopa de Pollo — Mexico City (an archeological find!)	soup
Tess Gallagher, p. 151	Pears a la Carver	pears in caramel sauce
James Galvin, p. 32	Fried Mush	cereal
Eugene K. Garber, p. 106	Zarzuela de Pescados	seafood
Christian Gehman, p. 154	Cake with Carrots	cake
Gary Gildner, p. 76	Golamki	stuffed cabbage
Louise Gluck, p. 77	Lenny's Hamburger	hamburger
Gail Godwin, p. 44	Carry Rivers' Cheese Souffle	cheese souffle
Herbert Gold, p. 32	Herbert Gold's Early Lunch	apples and cheese
Barry Goldensohn, p. 33	Bon Bon Chicken Sandwich	chicken sandwich
Jorie Graham, p. 77	Medieval Beef	beef
Francine du Plessix Gray, p. 155	Zabaglione Francesca	dessert
Doris Grumbach, p. 78	Writer's Outdoor Meal	barbeque
Joe Haldeman, p. 80	Boozy Beef (serves 4)	beef
Donald hall, p. 137	Spanish Eagle Rice	rice
Daniel Halpern, p. 122	Lamb Stew	stew
John Hawkes, p. 45	The High Cholesterol Breakfast	eggs/bacon/
Gwen Head, p. 54	Commuter's Pasta	pasta
Anthony Hecht, p. 81	Dolma for 5	beef casserole
Mark Helprin, p. 156	Lawrence of Arabia Rock Cake	cake
p. 10	Shrimp Bisque	shrimp
Don Hendrie Jr., p. 40	Marinade	marinade (sirloin)
Edward Hoagland, p. 124	Scrambled Eggs and Bear Stew Brunch with Bloody Marys	eggs/stew/ beverage
Jane Howard, p. 11	Chili	soup
David Hughes, p. 138	Cauliflower Polonaise	cauliflower
John Irving, p. 56	Pasta Sauce with Shrimp	pasta sauce

AUTHOR	TITLE	RECIPE
Laura Jensen, p. 83	My Grandmother's Beef Stew	stew
Donald Justice, p. 139	Avocado-Tomato Salad	salad
Edmund Keeley, p. 41	Keeley	beverage
George Keithley, p. 84	Beef and Beer Stew	stew
William Kennedy, p. 125	Roast Loin of Pork	port — roast loin
X.J. Kennedy, p. 157	Swinishly Creamy Chocolate Ice Cream	ice cream
Tracy Kidder, p. 22	English Muffins	muffins
Galway Kinnell, p. 139	Salad Dressing a la Sylvie	salad dressing
W.P. (Bill) Kinsella, p. 12	Bologna Soup	soup
Peter Klappert, p. 108	Live-Broiled Lobster	lobster
Maxine Kumin, p. 22	Squash Bread	squash bread
John Leggett, p. 110	John Leggett's Nostalgie de la Mer	seafood
Philip Levine, p. 141	Potato Pancakes (Latkes)	potato pancakes
Thomas Lux, p. 126	Barbeque Pork Ribs	pork ribs
Robie Macauley, p. 58	Pasta Boccaccio	pasta
Saul Maloff, p. 127	Stuffed Derma	bunget
p. 111	Gefilte Fish	fish
William Matthews, p. 85	Beef Salad	salad
James McPherson, p. 144	Sweet Potato Pie	sweet potato pie
Nicholas Meyer, p. 68	Cottage Cheese Enchiladas	enchiladas
Leonard Michaels, p. 34	Black Bread, Butter, Onion Coffee	sandwich
Bharati Mukherjee, p. 99	Bharati's Saffron and Yogurt Chicken	chicken
William Murray, p. 59	Spaghetti Irlandese	spaghetti
Carol Muske, p. 12	Cream of Zucchini Soup	soup
Peter Nelson, p. 13	Shadow Soup	soup
Howard Nemerov, p. 46	Eggs Maledict	eggs
Tim O'Orien, p. 24	Blueberry Muffins	muffins
Steve Orlen, p. 69	Renjilian Pilaf	pilaf
Grace Paley, p. 47	Souffle	souffle
p. 14	Soup	soup
Stanley Plumly, p. 60	Pasta Primavera (for two or three)	pasta

AUTHOR	TITLE	RECIPE
Reynolds Price, p. 47	Soft-Boiled Eggs	softboiled eggs
Vern Rutsala, p. 86	Rutsala's Main Dish	casserole
Michael Ryan, p. 48	Recipe for Sunday Morning (sans cockatoos)	eggs
Sherod Santos, p. 15	Portuguese Kale and Linguica Soup	soup
Charles Simic, p. 87	(Anecdote about his recipes being top secret)	
Jame Smiley, p. 100	Red Chicken With Herbs	chicken
W.D. Snodgrass, p. 16	K.B.'s Cold Blueberry Soup	soup
William Stafford, p. 25	Watching the Toast	poem on toast
Maura Stanton, p. 70	David's Enchiladas	enchiladas
Gerald Stern, p. 88	Jerry's Stew	stew
Richard Stern, p. 128	(Anecdote about not being a cook)	
Robert Stone, p. 17	Lentil Soup	soup
Mark Strand, p. 61	Spaghetti Carbonara	spaghetti
Mary Swander, p. 71	Tofu Tempura	tofu
Thom Swiss, p. 72	Curried Rice	rice
James Tate, p. 129	Squirrel Brains in Black Butter	squirrel
Anne Tyler, p. 35	Almost Infallible Cure for Writer's Block	peanut butter & jelly
Leslie Ullman, p. 36	Spinach Dip	dip
Doug Unger, p. 113	Salmon Joseph	salmon
Constance Urdang, p. 41	Blake's No-Cook Barbeque Sauce	barbeque sauce
Mona Van Duyn, p. 62	My Husband's Favorite Macaroni and Cheese Dish	macaroni and cheese
Arturo Vivante, p. 63	Pasta Sauce	pasta sauce
Dan Wakefield, p. 17	Essential Chili	soup
Paul West, p. 115	Sludge	seafood
Joy Williams, p. 26	Potato Bread with Caraway Seeds	bread
Miller Williams, p. 49	Eggs Fayetteville	eggs
Angus Wilson, p. 130	Pig's Feet	pig's feet
Robley Wilson Jr., p. 27	Peanut Butter Bread	bread
Hilma Wolitzer, p. 159	Chocolate Cake	cake
Charles & Holly Wright, p. 101	Holly's Quail	quali